The Hist

HAMILTON

Norfolk Brushmakers since 1746

Front Cover: A show case merchandiser of the late 1930s

Back Cover: The registered trade marks of the constituent companies of
Hamilton Acorn

Picture credits

The author and publishers wish to thank the following for kind permission
to reproduce illustrations: Harrow Museum and Heritage Centre for Plates
1, 19, 21, 23, 36; Norfolk Museum of Rural Life, Gressenhall, for Plates
2-4, 9-13, 17, 29, 42; Philip Yaxley for Plates 5, 6, 14, 15, 16, 38, 39, 41,
45, 46; Page Brothers Limited for Plate 7; Michael Marwood for Plate 33;
Mrs Elizabeth Ollier for Plate 34; Peter Chadwick for Plates 47, 48, 49;
Bob Clarke for Plate 26; Wymondham Heritage Museum for Plates 30, 32;
Gloria Ryder for Plates 43, 44; *Brushmaking* for Plates 20, 31; Hamilton
Acorn Limited for Plates 8, 18, 24, 25, 27, 28, 35, 37, 40, 50-52; Plan of
Wymondham factory, Wymondham Town Archives.

A BRUSH WITH HERITAGE

The History of
HAMILTON ACORN
Norfolk Brushmakers since 1746

Christine Clark

IBSN No 0 906219 41 8

Published for Hamilton Acorn by The Centre of East Anglian Studies, University of East Anglia

Printed and arranged by the printing unit, UEA, Norwich

Contents

List of illustrations figures and map

Figures

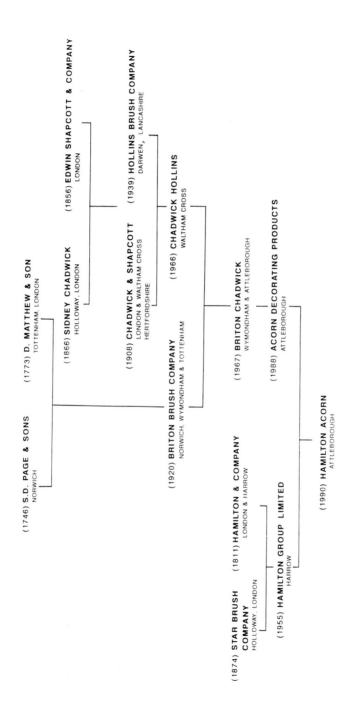

(1746) **S.D. PAGE & SONS**
NORWICH

(1773) **D. MATTHEW & SON**
TOTTENHAM, LONDON

(1856) **EDWIN SHAPCOTT & COMPANY**
LONDON

(1939) **HOLLINS BRUSH COMPANY**
DARWEN, LANCASHIRE

(1866) **SIDNEY CHADWICK**
HOLLOWAY, LONDON

(1908) **CHADWICK & SHAPCOTT**
LONDON & WALTHAM CROSS
HERTFORDSHIRE

(1966) **CHADWICK HOLLINS**
WALTHAM CROSS

(1920) **BRITON BRUSH COMPANY**
NORWICH, WYMONDHAM & TOTTENHAM

(1967) **BRITON CHADWICK**
WYMONDHAM & ATTLEBOROUGH

(1988) **ACORN DECORATING PRODUCTS**
ATTLEBOROUGH

(1874) **STAR BRUSH COMPANY**
HOLLOWAY, LONDON

(1811) **HAMILTON & COMPANY**
LONDON & HARROW

(1955) **HAMILTON GROUP LIMITED**
HARROW

(1990) **HAMILTON ACORN**
ATTLEBOROUGH

The companies forming Hamilton Acorn, 1746-1996

8

FOREWORD

The history of Hamilton Acorn is much more than just a fascinating chronicle which traces the development of the traditional craft business of brushmaking over two hundred and fifty years.

It is principally a story of people and their robust endeavour and determination to run and expand a series of businesses through changing times, turbulent economic peaks and troughs and persistent forces of competition. Among these people are the industry's early risk-takers, opportunists, skilled marketers, clever investors, resourceful engineers, sound planners and able tacticians. They impress with their focus, resolve and sheer professionalism: even more so when, particularly in the early days, all those talents were frequently needed on one pair of shoulders. All of them, managers and employees alike, have provided the company with a heritage that is built on the need by these successive generations to be best in the market.

This is in itself an awesome challenge to those of us working in the business on this special anniversary. Two hundred and fifty years is a remarkable milestone, achieved by very few in any industry and by no other in brushmaking. We were determined that it should be marked in an appropriate way. It is our belief that a thoroughly-researched history will be a proper tribute to the efforts of our predecessors and a permanent record for those taking the company forward. We trust you will enjoy reading it.

The name of the business may have changed many times over the years, but the underlying philosophy has not. Innovation is still a prime motivator both in products and processes. That requires judicious investment in marketing, machinery and systems. But we shall always continue to place due emphasis on the quality, service and craftsmanship that have been a key to success in the past.

Significant developments at Hamilton Acorn in recent times have introduced new products to make decorating easier for professional tradesmen and the do-it-yourself painter. Blends of man-made filaments have been introduced which replicate exactly the nature and qualities of traditional hog bristle for brushes. On rollers, new fabrics are now welded onto the core, instead of being glued, providing a tool that will cope with the rigours of hard work much better than before. There are now clever new applicators for the DIY market which provide maximum skill with the minimum of effort: again making the task simpler.

Our place in the market is strong, particularly so in the professional sector. This is due in no small part to the longevity and consistently high reputation of our two brands. Hamilton and Acorn have been recognised as providing the ultimate in decorating applicators for 185 years and 88 years respectively. Few products can claim such durable pedigrees. The people in our business today appreciate the wealth of tradition and sheer hard work that has been put into building these brands over time. They are also aware of the responsibility that this puts on all of us for the future.

We intend to celebrate with pride this anniversary with our customers, suppliers and industry colleagues, as well as our families and friends in the community of Norfolk. Then we shall step out with a clear intention to make the milestones ahead as worthy of record as those of the past.

Dennis Marrison
Managing Director
Hamilton Acorn, 1996

PREFACE

This book has been commissioned to celebrate 250 years of trading by the Norfolk brushmakers, Hamilton Acorn. The present-day company comprises several of Britain's best-known brushmaking firms: S.D. Page & Sons, of Norwich; the London companies, D. Matthew & Son, Hamilton & Company and the Star Brush Company; Chadwick & Shapcott of Waltham Cross in Hertfordshire and the Hollins Brush Company of Darwen, Lancashire (see the business tree on page 8). With the exception of the latter, all were old-established concerns. Notably, S.D. Page & Sons traces its origins back to 1746 when Samuel Deyns set up in business in the Haymarket, Norwich. Subsequently, the firm was owned and managed by six generations of Samuel's descendants. This itself was a rare achievement. Therefore, when in 1920 Pages merged with D. Matthew & Son to form the Briton Brush Company, the new firm brought together two of the oldest-known brushmaking concerns. Established in 1773, Matthews had similarly been owned by six generations of the same family. Likewise, Hamiltons (founded in 1811), Chadwick & Shapcott (founded 1856) and the Star Brush Company (founded 1874), were all built-up on a long tradition of family ownership.

In 1946, at the celebrations held to mark the 200th anniversary of the Briton Brush Company, one of its directors, Dr Cecil Page, a Fellow of the Society of Antiquaries and secretary of the Norfolk Record Society, pleaded with businessmen to preserve their company's records. He lamented the fact that few had been retained by his own firm. This is inevitably reflected in the book. As far as the sources allow, I have traced in some detail the history of Pages and the Briton Brush Company and, to a lesser extent, the other member-firms. The main focus is on the owners and their constant endeavours to adapt to changing and often difficult circumstances. To set their achievements in context, I have also considered the main developments within brushmaking and its transition from a regional craft to the modern-day industry. The result is a story of risk-taking, of innovation and, above all, a determination to survive.

I have received help and encouragement from many sources.

In particular I must mention David Pressley, marketing director of Lionheart plc, whose enthusiasm and support have ensured my task throughout has been enjoyable. John Cheston, Peter Chadwick, Bob Clarke, Douglas MacDonald, Michael Marwood and George Mabbutt, all past members of Hamilton Acorn, spared time to answer my questions and made many useful suggestions. Under the guidance of Dr Alec Douet of the Centre of East Anglian Studies, they pooled their memories to provide a lasting record of their many years of experience in brushmaking. Mrs Elizabeth Ollier provided details of the Page family pedigree. David Armstrong, managing director of Page Brothers Limited (printers), who until 1890 shared a common history with S.D. Page & Sons, kindly gave me access to his company's archives; this proved invaluable in writing the first chapter.

I should also like to express my thanks to Helen O'Hara of Harrow Museum and Heritage Centre; Frances Collinson of the Norfolk Museum of Rural Life, Gressenhall; Janet Smith of Wymondham Town Archives; Eric Thorburn of Wymondham Heritage Museum and Angus Nisbett, secretary of the British Hardware and Housewares Manufacturers' Association. Philip Yaxley, Richard Bartrum and Gloria Ryder generously allowed me to reproduce photographs from their collections. Mrs Dorothy Codd let me see her scrap-book of newspaper cuttings and David Cubitt provided me with genealogical details of the Page family. Phillip Judge of the School of Environmental Studies drew the map and plans and Michael Brandon-Jones of the School of World Art Studies and Museology expertly reproduced the illustrations. Mavis Wesley prepared the final manuscript and kindly answered my many queries.

I owe an especial debt to Dr Richard Wilson, Director of the Centre of East Anglian Studies, who has read and commented upon my work. With his usual patience and good humour, he has rescued me from a number of inaccuracies and inconsistencies. Finally, I should like to thank my keenest critic, my husband, Robin. I am grateful to them all.

Christine Clark
University of East Anglia

CHAPTER I

Brushmaking in Norwich and the Early Years
of S.D. Page & Sons

The history of the present-day company of Hamilton Acorn begins in eighteenth-century Norwich where Samuel Deyns (1722-1806) founded a small basket-making enterprise.[1] We know little of Samuel's early years, but in 1736 he was apprenticed to John Dunn, basket maker, of St John Maddermarket and seven years later on 3 May 1743, he became a Freeman of the City of Norwich. In 1746 when Francis Allen, a well-established basket maker and osier grower, acquired new premises at 4 Haymarket, he is believed to have taken young Samuel into partnership. Subsequently, Samuel set up his own business at St Andrew's Plain and, after Allen's death in 1762, purchased his Haymarket property. It was here that for at least twenty years Samuel lived with his wife and young family, manufacturing and selling his wares. His business, although still small, was firmly established: he retained and rented the St Andrew's property, acquired land at Thorpe and became an Alderman of the city. And local directories show that by 1802 he had acquired larger premises at 23 Haymarket which were to remain for more than a century the headquarters of the family firm.

At some point Samuel extended his basket-making business to include that of brushmaking.[2] The choice was scarcely surprising, for the two crafts had long been closely associated. Moreover, it is clear that by the end of the eighteenth century Norwich was already an established centre of the trade. The receipts for grants of freedom indicate there were master brushmakers in the city throughout the eighteenth century and *The Directory of Norwich, 1783*, lists three established firms; by 1822 the number had risen to ten and, by 1845, to sixteen.[3] The growing importance of Norwich in the national trade is confirmed by the records of the United Society of Brushmakers, formed in 1747. The Society's main objective was to provide support for unemployed journeymen who 'tramped' the circuit of the main brushmaking towns seeking employment. At the clubhouse of each of its branches - in Norwich it was at the York Tavern in Castle Ditches - members received a bed, beer and an allowance to sustain them on the next stage of their journey. By 1829, the tramping route featured five East Anglian outposts: Ipswich, Bury St Edmunds, Diss, Norwich and King's Lynn. A decade later the Society distributed to all its members a newly designed emblem which, besides its own trade arms, depicted the coats of arms of the seven major brushmaking centres, among them, Norwich.[4]

The position of Norwich and, indeed, Norfolk, at the forefront of brushmaking, was undoubtedly underpinned by the county's abundant supply of timber, especially in the southern wood-pasture region. Until the mid-nineteenth century, almost the only raw materials used in brushmaking were Russian bristle, horsehair, whalebone (which was finely cut and used as a filling for stiff brooms and brushes) and the wooden stocks which were turned and cut from local timber. Because of its hardness and fine grain, the most popular wood was beech. Alder and birch were favoured for brooms, but a wide variety, including oak, elm, chestnut, sycamore and cherry, was used. Few areas were better endowed than south Norfolk. By the early seventeenth century, the town of Wymondham, nine miles south-west of Norwich, was a noted centre of woodturning, a specialisation based on the fine quality of the native wood. A century later, the Norfolk historian, Francis Blomefield, described the area as '[abounding] with a good quantity of Wood and Timber'[5] It was from Wymondham that subsequent generations of Samuel's family obtained their brush stocks and in later years the town was the natural choice for the company's further expansion. And while increasing quantities of timber, especially Norwegian birch, were imported, the region remained the major source of supply until well into the twentieth century. As the company's 1930s handbook, mindful to stress its dependence upon home-produced materials, confirmed: 'there are few counties to equal [Norfolk's] magnificent woodlands ... there is no wood like the Norfolk beech.'[6]

The extension of Samuel's interests was not only a means of consolidating his enterprise but also a common response to the vagaries of the economic climate. Nevertheless, for many years his firm's continuation must have seemed uncertain, for the great sadness

Plate 1   Horace, the wild boar, who for many years graced reception at the Harrow factory. Wild boars provide the bristle which remains a major raw material for brushmaking.

of Samuel's life was the death, at the age of thirteen, of his only son and heir.   However, through his daughter, Elizabeth, who on 8 August 1780 married John Page of Attlebridge, he secured the succession of the business.   The Page family originated from Walsham le Willows in Suffolk.   Around 1700, John's grandfather, Philip I, settled at Hall Farm, Attlebridge, subsequently acquiring the neighbouring farm and further property at Hindolveston. Unfortunately his elder son, Philip II, dissipated much of his inheritance; the farms were sold and his sons, John and Philip III, continued as tenants.   John, like his father, was a spendthrift and on his marriage to Elizabeth, Samuel Deyns not only provided a handsome dowry but also settled his new son-in-law's debts.   But Samuel, then almost sixty, attached one condition: that the first son of the marriage should enter his firm.   Thus Samuel Deyns Page (1782-1845), born two years later, went as a child to live in Norwich and was duly apprenticed to his grandfather.[7]   In 1803, on coming of age, he became a partner in the firm and on Samuel's death three years later inherited his business interests.[8]

The young man's prospects had already been augmented by his marriage in 1805 to Sarah, the only surviving child of Sarah and Martin Fountain.   A member of the Norwich Corporation and Sheriff in 1812, Martin Fountain was a prosperous builder who worked on

Plate 2   Samuel Deyns (1720-1806), the founder of S.D. Page & Sons.

Plate 3   Samuel Deyns Page (1782-1845), Samuel Deyns' grandson and the stalwart of John and Elizabeth Page's large family.

Plate 4   Samuel Deyns Page (1810-1897), senior partner in S.& D. Page & Sons, 1845-1876.

many civic buildings including the shirehall, the city gaol and the new cavalry barracks. And on his death in 1828 Samuel II inherited his considerable property in the parish of St Mary.[9] The support of his well-to-do father-in-law may well have been instrumental to the survival of the firm. For these were difficult years; the end of the French Wars in 1815 brought the collapse of cereal prices and deep depression to the rural economy, and the failure of small businesses was commonplace. But the little we know of Samuel's affairs suggests he used his resources to good effect. One response to the uncertain climate was further diversification to include the manufacture of wooden pattens and wholesale stationery and drapery.[10] His three sons also received a sound business training. Samuel III (1810-1897), the third of Samuel and Sarah's nine children, was apprenticed to his father and in 1831 became a partner in the firm which was subsequently restyled S.D. Page & Son. His second son, Martin, was apprenticed to a Chelmsford ironmonger before setting up in business at Orford Hill, Norwich, while John was apprenticed to a stationer at Wells-next-the-sea. And Samuel participated fully in civic life, serving as councillor for Mancroft ward in 1813 and 1821-25. During the Chartist riots, he volunteered as a special constable and was responsible for the arrest of one of the ringleaders. Nevertheless, he enjoyed a reputation as a kind and just employer. Samuel's progress is all the more notable because of the six sons of John and Elizabeth Page, he alone prospered. Indeed, on more than one occasion he was called on to rescue his feckless brothers, Henry, an ironmonger at Fakenham, who turned forger and fled to Ireland and John Gymor, who ran off to Antigua leaving his wife and three young daughters to support themselves.[11]

Certainly, by his death in 1845, Samuel had steered the business through some of the most challenging years of the nineteenth century. In contrast, when Samuel III took control, the climate was altogether more optimistic. Three factors were of particular importance. First, the long depression which had hung like a pall over East Anglia for almost thirty years was at last easing. Second was the purchase of the neighbouring property at 22 Haymarket which fell vacant shortly before his father's death. This had effectively doubled the size of the factory and enabled the main departments to be extended. Brushmaking, in particular, was steadily superseding the manufacture of baskets. Wrapping papers, twines and string were also factored while a new venture was the manufacture of customised paper bags, mainly for confectioners and grocers. Initially, these were hand made, but soon three steam-powered machines were introduced which, according to Bayne, 'pasted, folded and completed [each bag] with astonishing rapidity.'[12] Finally, small printing machines were added in order to print bill heads, statements and invoices. The third factor was the completion in 1845 of the Norfolk and Eastern Counties Railway line from Norwich, via Ely and Cambridge, to London. Until that time, most of the company's trade was local. One hard-pressed traveller covered the towns and larger villages of Norfolk and Suffolk, but the difficulties and cost of transporting bulky goods by local carrier prevented wider expansion. The coming of the railways suddenly provided the opportunity to sell in the national market. Trade grew steadily, and two further travellers were soon employed to cover the Midlands and Southern Counties and agents appointed in London and the more distant North of England, Scotland and Ireland.

During these years, family interests were further strengthened when on 9 October 1835, Samuel III married his cousin, Elizabeth Frances, eldest daughter of John Gymor Page, who had returned from the West Indies penniless and, we must assume, repentant for he was by now an established member of the company. During the next thirteen years, the couple were blessed with seven sons and two daughters. The eldest son, Samuel IV (b.1836), was destined to enter the business but, unable to settle, eventually emigrated to Canada. In his place, the second son, Frederick John (1838-1927), was trained by his father to manage the brushmaking department while his younger brother, Charles Fountain (1839-1921), worked his way through the remaining departments - paper-bag making, printing, accounts and sales.[13]

When in 1860 Frederick and Charles became partners in S.D. Page & Sons, the firm was already outgrowing its premises. To a large extent this reflected the radical changes affecting brushmaking at this time. For several reasons - the economic recovery after the mid-1840s, the headlong growth of towns and cities of all descriptions and the greater understanding of the importance of sanitation - the demand for brushes of all types was rising rapidly.

Equally important, just as the scarcity and high price of Russian bristle threatened expansion, a wide range of vegetable fibres which were to revolutionise the trade were beginning to make their appearance.[14] The first, Bahia bass, so named after the port in North Brazil from which it originated, was introduced in the 1840s. Obtained from the bark of local palms, for years the fibre was used as packing around bags of sugar. Exactly how its potential for brushmaking was discovered remains unclear, but it was slowly adopted for the manufacture of the low-cost brooms to which it gave its name.[15] The real breakthrough, however, came a decade later with the arrival of Mexican fibre, a cheap and versatile substitute for bristle which was quickly adopted throughout the trade. Other new materials followed: kitool, bassine, African, Madagascar and Coco fibres with the result that many brushes could be manufactured and sold more cheaply. Indeed, the combination of the buoyant market and the new range of raw materials tempted many newcomers to enter the trade, mostly selling low-cost goods to the wholesale warehouses which proliferated in the major cities. But for the larger, well-established companies, a further opportunity beckoned when many of them quickly established a flourishing export trade, especially with the Colonies and the USA.[16]

Against this favourable background Pages expanded rapidly. During the 1860s an extension was built at right angles to the Haymarket factory to house the engine and boiler house, bass and fibre dressing shops and stores. Whereas in 1851 Samuel had employed a total of twenty-two men, by the end of the 1860s Bayne reckoned that over a hundred were employed in brushmaking alone.[17] The factory was further enlarged in 1872 when the adjoining charity school, built in 1723, was demolished. Pages had become an important firm in Norwich, inhabitants and visitors alike constantly reminded of its smokey presence by the scale and activity of its city-centre site. About this time, the decision was also taken to discontinue the production of pattens and to concentrate solely on brushmaking, stationery and printing. A few years later, the offices and paper stocks were moved to leased premises in Theatre Street some fifty metres from the Haymarket (see the map showing the company's premises on page 21). The paper-bag making machinery and printing machines were moved to the basement and in their place a new department manufacturing paintbrushes was established at the main factory. The catalogue of 1880, the earliest to have survived, illustrates the wide variety of brushes, ranging from bass brooms and deck scrubs to fine sable pencils and ornate hearth brushes,

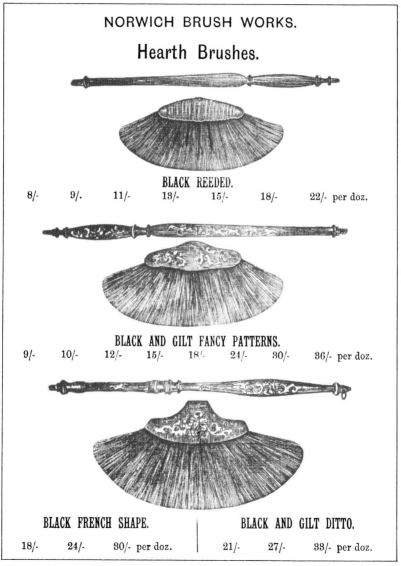

Plate 5 A range of hearth brushes from the 1880 catalogue of S.D. Page & Sons.

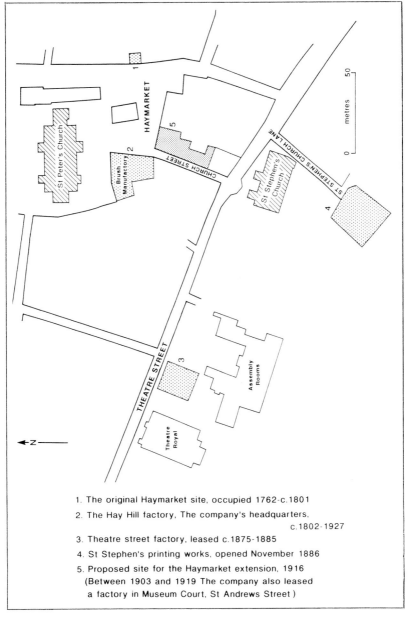

1. The original Haymarket site, occupied 1762-c.1801
2. The Hay Hill factory, The company's headquarters,
   c.1802-1927
3. Theatre street factory, leased c.1875-1885
4. St Stephen's printing works, opened November 1886
5. Proposed site for the Haymarket extension, 1916
   (Between 1903 and 1919 The company also leased
   a factory in Museum Court, St Andrews Street)

S.D. Page & Sons' Norwich premises, 1762-1927.

manufactured both for home and export markets. The whole of England and Wales were regularly covered by five travellers together with a network of agents scattered across Scotland and Ireland. Similarly, exports were organised in conjunction with a Sheffield

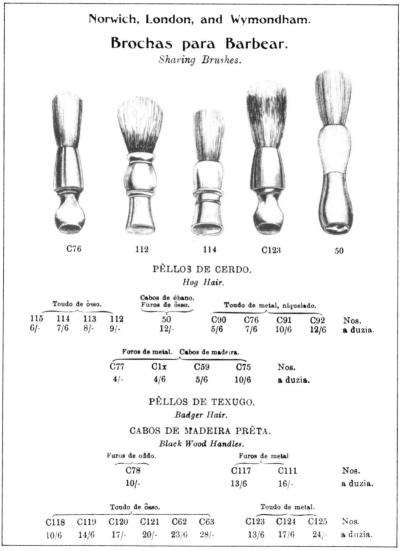

Norwich, London, and Wymondham.

Brochas para Barbear.

Shaving Brushes.

| C76 | 112 | 114 | C123 | 50 |

PÊLLOS DE CERDO.
Hog Hair.

	Toudo de ôsso.			Cabos de ébano. Furos de ôsso.		Toudo de metal, niquelado.			
115	114	113	112	50	C90	C76	C91	C92	Nos.
6/-	7/6	8/-	9/-	12/-	5/6	7/6	10/6	12/6	a duzia.

	Furos de metal.	Cabos de madeira.			
C77	C1x	C59	C75	Nos.
4/-	4/6	5/6	10/6	a duzia.

PÊLLOS DE TEXUGO.
Badger Hair.

CABOS DE MADEIRA PRÊTA.
Black Wood Handles.

Furos de oddo.		Furos de metal		
C78		C117	C111	Nos.
10/-		13/6	16/-	a duzia.

	Toudo de ôsso.					Toudo de metal.			
C118	C119	C120	C121	C62	C63	C123	C124	C125	Nos.
10/6	14/6	17/-	20/-	23/6	28/-	13/6	17/6	24/-	a duzia.

Plate 6   Shaving brushes for the Brazilian trade, from S.D. Page & Sons' 1905 export catalogue.

cutlery firm and a Birmingham manufacturer of agricultural tools. The three companies between them employed a wearily peripatetic Mr Fry, who sold their products on a commission basis, one year travelling through South Africa, Australia, New Zealand and China, the next, through Canada, the United States and South America.[18] Large contracts to supply local authorities and the armed forces provided another important market. Indeed, there is no doubt that by the early 1880s the company enjoyed a reputation as one of the country's leading brushmakers.

The growth of the printing department was equally rapid. In particular, the introduction of lithography, which facilitated colour printing, brought commissions for catalogues, posters and hand-bills from many city firms. Expansion, however, brought its own problems. For despite the additions and alterations, the city-centre site (valued a few years later at only £6,100), with its workforce approaching three hundred, was becoming increasingly congested.[19] Moreover, fronting the Haymarket and confined on the remaining three sides by roads and buildings (see plate 7, page 24), further expansion was out of the question. It was decided, therefore, to replace the leased warehouse with a purpose-built printing works. A suitable site was found behind St Stephens church close to the Haymarket. A number of derelict cottages were demolished and a modern, two-storey factory, with power supplied by a large Crossley gas engine connected to the city main, and incorporating a well-lit artist's studio, was completed in November 1886. Notably, one of the first apprentices to be trained as a lithographic artist with the firm in the 1890s was the young Alfred Munnings, the well-known artist and future President of the Royal Academy.

The opening of the St Stephen's printing works marked the first stage in the division of the family business. The old partnership was dissolved and two new companies formed, the name of S.D. Page & Sons being retained by the brushmaking side of the business, with Page Brothers & Company representing the printing interests. Initially the changes made little difference to the management of the overall business, except that Samuel III, having retired from active work in 1876, now withdrew completely. Frederick continued to manage the brushworks while Charles took charge of the new factory and maintained his responsibility for the finances and sales policy of

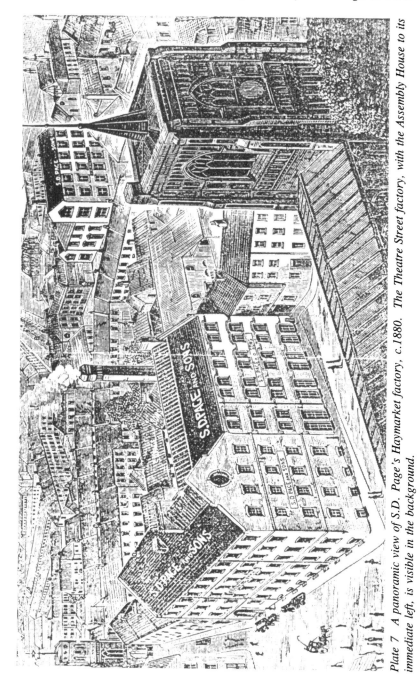

Plate 7   A panoramic view of S.D. Page's Haymarket factory, c.1880.   The Theatre Street factory, with the Assembly House to its immediate left, is visible in the background.

the two companies. Barely four years later, however, the *London Gazette* gave notice that:

> The partnership carried on by Frederick John Page
> and Charles Fountain Page ... has been dissolved, as
> from the 12th day of April last, by mutual consent.
> Dated this 31st day of December 1890.[20]

From that time onwards there was no further connection between the two businesses. What was perhaps surprising was the announcement by Frederick that he would 'no longer have an interest in the Brush Business, but will give his personal attention exclusively to the Paper and Printing Trades.'[21] And when in March 1891 the firm of S.D. Page & Sons, wholesale brush manufacturers and merchants, was registered as a private limited company with a capital of £30,000, it was Charles who became its first managing director.[22] The explanation is to be found in the difficulties facing not only S.D. Page & Sons, but brushmaking in general, during the 1880s. To these events, which were to test family relationships and the very survival of the firm, we must now turn.

NOTES

1. Information about the origins of S.D. Page & Sons is taken from the notes of H.W. Earl (1979) of Page Brothers Limited, Revd Reginald Page, 'A Family History' (typescript, 1910) and E. Burgess, *Men Who Have Made Norwich,* (1904), pp. 142-153. I am also grateful to Mr David Cubitt for genealogical references and information about Martin Fountain.

2. It is unclear exactly when Samuel Deyns began brushmaking. In early trade directories (1783, 1794 and 1802) he is listed only as basketmaker, and in his will, written 26 July 1805, he describes himself as 'Basketmaker'. However, in the codicil added less than a month later, he calls himself 'Brushmaker', suggesting that he may previously have been involved in the trade.

3. City Treasurer's Accounts of Receipts for Grants of Freedom; William Chase, *Directory of Norwich,* 1783; Pigot and Company, *National Commercial Directory,* 1822-23; William White, *History, Gazetteer and Directory of Norfolk,* 1845.

4.   The seven were: London, Manchester, Leeds, Birmingham, Bristol, Sheffield and Norwich. By 1895, approximately 16,000 were employed in the trade, almost 5,000 in London. The other main centres were: Birmingham, 899; Norwich, 653; Manchester, 422; Walsall, 404; Bristol, 332 and Sheffield, 324; William Kiddier, *The Old Trade Unions: From the Unprinted Records of the Brushmakers,* (1930), pp. 13-21, 50-1, 237-8; *The Brush Journal,* Vol.I, March 1895, pp. 1-4.

5.   Joan Thirsk (ed.), *The Agrarian History of England and Wales 1500-1640,* Vol. IV, (Cambridge, 1967) pp.427, 496; Quoted in Philip Yaxley, *Memories of Old Wymondham,* (1985), p. 18.

6.   *The Briton Brush Company Limited,* (1933), p. 6; When supplies of imported timber were cut off during World War One, it was the proximity of many well-stocked timber estates which attracted the Co-operative Wholesale Society to Wymondham. In 1917 the company purchased the Poynt sawmills from George Semmence & Sons. Initially brush stocks were manufactured for the Leeds factory, but in 1922 a new factory was built on the thirteen acre site. The factory, which at its peak employed over 200, closed in 1983; Mary Manning, 'The Co-operative Wholesale Society Brushworks, Wymondham', *The Journal of the Norfolk Archaeology Society* (1983).

7.   Revd Reginald Page, 'A Family History', pp. 1-4.

8.   Samuel also inherited his grandfather's land at Thorpe and £300; his mother, Elizabeth Page, received the property at St Andrew's Plain and small bequests were left to Samuel's other grandchildren ; Will of Samuel Deyns, proved 28 June 1806.

9.   T. Hawes (ed.), 'An Index to Norwich City Officers, 1453-1835', *Norfolk Genealogy,* Vol. 21, (1989) p. 62; *Norwich Mercury,* 6 July 1822; Will of Martin Fountain, proved 1828.

10.   The earliest indication of an interest in stationery and the manufacture of pattens (wooden platforms with straps, designed to keep the wearer's shoes dry and clean) and clogs - a trade commonly associated with brushmaking - is in Pigot & Company, *National Commercial Directory,* 1822-3. Wholesale drapery is mentioned only between 1836-45, but the Page family may have had a more enduring association with the trade. It is notable that Elizabeth Page inherited her father's property in St Andrew's Plain and that from the 1830s several directories list Page & Sons, St Andrew's Plain, Drapers, Tailors etc.

11. T. Hawes (ed.), 'Index to Norwich City Officers', p. 115; Revd Reginald Page, 'A Family History', pp. 3-4.

12. A.D. Bayne, *An Account of the Industry and Trade of Norwich and Norfolk,* (1869). p. 620.

13. Two of the children died in childhood. Edward (1844-1917) and John became sheep farmers in Australia, a third entered the church; Edward Bailey Page, 'A History of the Family Business', (typescript, 1949); Registers of St Peter Mancroft.

14. In subsequent years China became an important supplier of bristle and, to a lesser extent, India, although Russia was considered to supply the finest quality.

15. Bahia bass was one of a number of fibres obtained from the bark, stems or leaves of the palm family. A second important group of fibres were the whisks which were obtained from the roots of grasses, mainly imported from France and Mexico. For a more detailed discussion of the raw materials used in brushmaking, see M.R. Snow, *Brushmaking: Craft and Industry,* (1984). The process of brushmaking is explained below p. 30.

16. 'The Brush Trade During the Queen's Reign', *The Brush Journal,* Vol.III, June 1897, pp. 49-50.

17. Census return, 1851; A.D.Bayne, *Industry and Trade of Norwich,* p. 620.

18. Edward Bailey Page, 'History', p. 2.

19. Valuation of the Haymarket property, November 1893.

20. *London Gazette,* 3 February 1891.

21. Handbill, Page Brothers & Company, 14 April 1890.

22. S.D. Page & Sons Limited, Memorandum and Articles of Association, 2 March 1891.

CHAPTER II

Mechanisation and Expansion, 1880-1914

After two prosperous decades, the difficulties after 1880 came as a sharp shock to brushmakers everywhere. In part, they reflected the general stagnation of trade known as the Great Depression. More serious was the growing self-sufficiency of some colonies, at least in the manufacture of low-cost household brushes, and the flood of imports penetrating the domestic market.[1] Again, these were cheap goods, such as dandy and scrubbing brushes, made mainly in Germany and Belgium where labour costs were below those in Britain.[2] Here most workshops, for they hardly merited the description of factory, were situated in villages and relied heavily on 'out-workers'. In Saxony, in the Black Forest region, for instance, peasants collected supplies of drilled boards and filling from the workshop in the autumn, and returned in the spring to deliver brushes and collect payment.[3] The real challenge, however, came from foreign prison-made brushes - one of a range of products, including matting, printed and knitted goods - manufactured using 'free' labour and then dumped in Britain. Not only were brushes sold at prices well below the cost of manufacture in Britain (£1.20 for a gross of scrubbing brushes against £1.57), but also many reputable British companies found their samples were sent abroad, copied and then sold as the genuine article. By 1895, when the government finally responded with a Departmental Committee enquiring into imports of prison-made goods, a number of firms had already been forced out of business.[4]

At Pages, the first sign of trouble was in the early 1880s when the travellers found their sales were undermined by imported goods. Week by week they returned with reduced order books and evidence of counterfeiting: brushes identical to their own, to the extent they were stamped with the firm's British manufacturer's identification number. In response, every attempt was made to reduce costs and, therefore, prices. Wages were cut. The company already employed a substantial proportion of women whose wages were well below those of men, but to cut costs further, out-working, a practice which had virtually disappeared, was re-introduced. Despite these efforts, the position worsened and soon only the profits from the printing department supported the overall business. Unfortunately, neither the partners' minutes nor accounts have survived to tell the full story, but to quote later generations, 'the company faced the most critical time in its history.'[5] Indeed, there is little doubt that had the controversial step of mechanising production not been taken, the business would not have survived.

Until the last quarter of the nineteenth century, brushes were hand-made and the only machines used were saws, lathes (worked by treadle) and drills for cutting, turning and boring the stocks and handles. The methods of manufacture had changed little over the centuries. Apprentices first learnt the intricacies of 'drawn-work', whereby wire was used to draw 'knots' of filling through bored stocks.[6] Once this was mastered, they moved on to 'pan-work', an older, but more difficult process, where the knots were set in the stock by using hot pitch. The work was highly-skilled and traditionally brushmakers were paid on a piecework basis. For most of the nineteenth century, the rate for pan-work was twenty knots a penny (less than half a new pence), which amounted to 4s 6d (22.5 pence) for a dozen good quality brooms of ninety knots.[7] At times of recession rates were cut, especially outside London, but attempts in 1829-33 to introduce women on half-pay were resisted so strongly by the National Society of Brushmakers, that it was not until the boom of the 1870s that the employment of women, mainly for drawn-work, became commonplace.[8] Overall, wages varied considerably reflecting individual skills, but in 1895 Charles Page suggested 40-70 pence a week for girls and women and £1, ranging to £1.75 for the highest skilled paintbrush workers, for men, rates similar to those paid by other witnesses to the Departmental Committee.[9]

From the early 1850s, a growing list of patents marked the slow shift towards mechanisation. These included a process for putting bristles through a perforated template into a wooden stock; another whereby a bundle of bristles was fastened by a wire staple and driven into the stocks.[10] But the real breakthrough came in 1869 when two young Americans, Edward Bradley and J. Sheldon, arrived in England with designs for a revolutionary machine for making solid-backed brushes.[11] Capable of fastening more than 100 knots a minute into pre-bored stocks and of boring the stocks in a single operation, the combined process marked a major step forward in brushmaking technology. Perhaps not surprisingly, the young men were unable to sell their machines to a conservative brushmaking community. However, with the financial backing of three agricultural engineers, Ransomes of Ipswich, Daniel Pidgeon of the Britannia Works at Banbury and Alfred Crosskill of Beverley, in Yorkshire, they formed J. Sheldon & Company and in 1871 opened a small brushmaking factory in Leather Lane, London. Despite many teething troubles, the machine-made brushes were inexpensive and strong, therefore slowly gaining in popularity. Disaster for the young firm struck, however, early in 1874, the entire factory being destroyed by fire. Sheldon returned to America but, with renewed support from his backers, Bradley built a new factory at the Metropolitan Cattle Market at Holloway and that same July, the business, renamed the Star Brush Company, was registered as a private limited liability company with Robert Ransome as its first chairman. Gradually, Bradley extended the range of machine-made brushes, all of which were stamped with the company's trade mark - the six-pointed star. He also pioneered high-speed woodworking machines for shaping brushbacks and machines to handle raw fibre. The company flourished. In only twelve years it had outgrown its premises and in November 1887 moved to a two acre site adjoining Holloway station. By the time Edward Bradley gave evidence to the Departmental Committee on prison-made imports in 1890, he was employing three hundred hands. The majority were girls and boys who operated his various machines, each of which he calculated was able to do the work of ten men.[12]

Despite the success of the Star Brush Company, only two firms immediately followed their lead: Webbs (later Webb & Foulger Limited), who in 1878 similarly built a factory for making brushes by machinery, and Pages, where the decision to introduce machines was taken only after much heart-searching and disagreement between the partners. With men of such different personalities, this was perhaps inevitable. Frederick, who had spent his entire working-life in the brush factory, was an austere and obstinate character who resisted change. Charles, who besides managing the printing works,

Plate 8 The 4.75 H.P. Daimler Wagonette, bought by Edward Bradley in 1898 and believed to be the second earliest trade van in London.

handled the firm's finances and sales, was exactly the opposite. An ambitious and progressive man, he was clearly the driving force behind the business. He single-handedly pushed through the economies at Norwich and finally, after much debate, persuaded his brother that they should introduce machines. At first they had little success, an American 'Woodbury' and a 'Bradley' both proving unsatisfactory. Then in 1885, the French engineer, J.V. Gane, came to London to demonstrate the filling machines he had designed and patented. Charles was so impressed he immediately bought the British and Colonial rights at a cost of £16,850.[13] At such an uncertain time this was a large outlay, especially with Frederick less than half-hearted in his approval. Moreover, Gane provided only one machine with its accompanying drawings. Five more were delivered from Paris at a cost of £100 each, and Burrells of Thetford

Plate 9   Charles Fountain Page (1839-1921), who was responsible for the rapid growth of S.D. Page & Sons after 1880.

Plate 10   Edward Bailey Page (1875-1958), Charles Page's third son, a talented engineer and instrumental in the merger with D. Matthew & Son in 1920.

Plate 11 Dr Cecil Page (1879-1951), a general practitioner until 1919, he took responsibility for the health and welfare of the workforce at Wymondham.

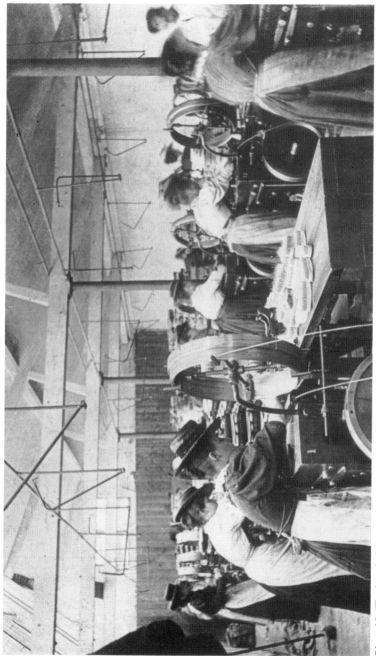

Plate 12 The brush-filling room at Wymondham 1901. The women are operating the machines patented by the French engineer, J.V. Gane, and introduced by the company in 1886

made another fifteen. However, as they had never before seen a filling machine, and as some of the specialist parts were made by the French engineers, Rochegude, at Montferneil near Paris, no two machines were exactly alike and there was great difficulty in getting them to work. Years later, as Edward Page, Charles' son, recalled, it was commonplace to find folded paper packed between the parts to ensure their smooth running.[14]

Besides the technical problems, there was also resistance to the introduction of machines from the drawing hands and foremen. Therefore, it was decided to open a small brushworks at the nearby market town of Wymondham, well away from the main factory.[15] Here, at a time of deep agricultural recession, there was no shortage of labour. Women were only too willing to walk in from the surrounding villages to find employment. And, of course, in contrast to Norwich's crowded city-centre, land was cheap and plentiful. Initially, the factory was little more than a row of cottages facing Lady's Lane,[16] but by the end of 1886, Gane's filling machines and a number of boring machines were installed and in operation. A sawmill and turnery were also built which supplied all the stocks and handles used in the two factories.

However, Page's problems were by no means over. In early 1890, just as the local press was complementing the company on its 'judicious management' and listing the factory among the many improvements to Wymondham, it was almost completely destroyed by fire.[17] No sooner was it rebuilt - the plans for a new two-storey factory were already under consideration - than the company was caught up in the wave of strikes which gripped Norwich throughout much of 1890-91. The problems began in June when 6,000 shoeworkers struck over piece-work rates. In December, attempts by Haldenstein's, one of the largest employers, to cut rates, precipitated a bitter, nine-week strike. And when in January 1891 Pages installed new boring machines in the Norwich factory and brought in piece-work rates which effectively cut wages by 12-15 per cent, members of the Amalgamated Society of Brushworkers came out on strike and were dismissed. The situation was exacerbated when the women at Wymondham, upon discovering they received lower pay than those in Norwich, joined the strike. In March, a demonstration in Norwich involved no fewer than 6,000 people. As a result the skilled men

Plate 13 Preparing brush-backs and stocks at Wymondham, 1901

were reinstated but several of the women were locked out until October without financial support from the union.[18] The strike, a rare occurrence in brushmaking, left a legacy of bitterness on both sides, and it was many years before the company again employed union members.[19]

It was against this background, then, that in April 1890 the brothers finally dissolved their partnership and Charles Page took control of the brushworks. Less than a year later, the firm was incorporated to facilitate further expansion and, doubtless, to gain the benefit of limited liability. Between 1892 and 1907, a total of £40,000 was raised by debentures while in 1908 the original capital of £30,000 was increased to £35,000 and the following year, to £65,000.[20] Charles Page became life-managing director and was joined on the board by Martin Fountain Page (1838-1903), the great-great-grandson of Philip Page II and senior partner of Page & Turner (corn, coal and cake merchants) of Blakeney, and Robert Bagshaw, a Norwich JP and alderman. Edward Bailey Page (1875-1958), the third of Charles' four talented sons - Reginald (1872-1953) entered the church while his two brothers, Algernon (1874-1946) and Cecil (1879-1951) trained in medicine - followed his father into the

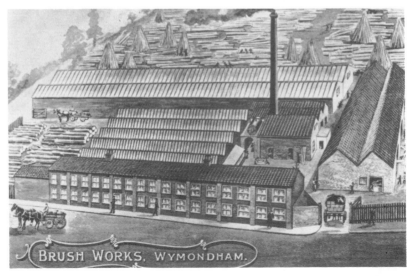

Plate 14 S.D. Page & Sons' factory at Lady's Lane, Wymondham in 1899, twice rebuilt after the fires of 1890 and 1894.

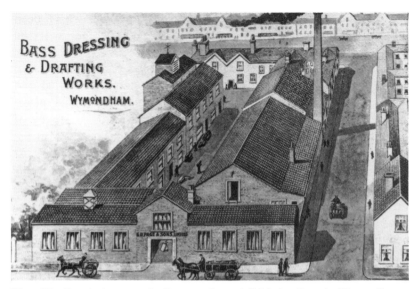

Plate 15 Cann's brewery, in Brewery Lane (off Market Street), Wymondham, leased from Morgan's Brewery Company of Norwich, 1896-1921, and converted into a bass dressing and drafting works.

business and joined the board in 1897 when, after a serious stroke, Martin Page retired.[21]

In March 1894, the company suffered a further blow when the Wymondham factory was again severely damaged by fire. In the view of the local press a 'strange ill-luck [seemed] to hang over the premises.'[22] But in reality, the difficulties of the preceding years had been largely overcome. The factory was rebuilt and extended (see plate 14), and when the following year Charles Page gave evidence to the Departmental Committee, the progress made by the company was there for all to see. The workforce numbered around 500, of whom 200 were employed at Wymondham, where there were now thirty filling machines. Each, he reckoned, could do the work of twelve drawing hands, enabling the firm to compete with the cheapest prison-made imports. For example, scrubbing brushes could be made for 96 pence or less against £1.57 a gross for hand made ones. He had sympathy with his fellow brushmakers. He joined them in their protest against unfair competition which depressed all prices and meant they could not recoup the cost of their patents. But, he firmly believed, their business would have been ruined had they not invested in machinery. As he emphasised: 'we did invest, and now we are stronger than before'.[23]

Thereafter, the business went from strength to strength. In 1896, Cann's Wymondham brewery was leased and converted into a bass dressing and drafting works to supply both factories (see plate, page 38).[24] Eight years later, Edmund Burgess, in his survey of leading Norwich companies, noted: 'an enormous increase [in the brush trade] in consequence of the introduction of machinery.' At Wymondham, 'where old fashioned hand methods are left far behind', he counted more than fifty filling machines, besides those for boring boards and backs. The saw mill and turnery were also totally mechanised while the research and engineering department, begun in 1890, boasted six engineers who, besides repairs, designed and manufactured new machines.[25] Shortly after the visit, the Wymondham site was again extended and that same year, a third factory was opened in the old printing works of the Norfolk News Company at Museum Court off St Andrew's Street, Norwich.[26]

Plate 16 The Wymondham dressing and drafting factory, c.1900.

Despite the rapid progress made by Pages, however, the economic climate remained difficult until World War One. The general recovery of trade from the mid-1890s was shortlived and from the turn of the century disputes within Russia and Poland

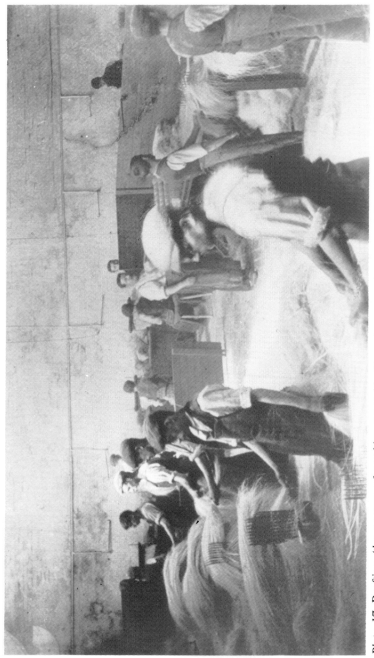

Plate 17 Drafting (the process of combing vegetable fibres to remove loose material) at Wymondham in 1901. Dressed fibres were then bound and cut to the lengths required for various domestic brushes.

caused an acute shortage of bristle and prices soared. Most importantly, imports, which increased from 1.1 million dozen brushes in 1900 to 1.9 million in 1913, caused persistent problems.[27] Indeed, the 1906 general election, fought mainly over free trade, brought widespread protest. The columns of the *Eastern Daily Press,* for example, recorded a bitter local debate between the two major political parties with brush workers warned that unless they voted for the Tories and protection they would soon be unemployed.[28] The following year saw the first moves towards collective action when in June, thirty-two firms met at the Great Eastern Hotel in London to agree a general increase in brush prices. From this came the suggestion for a 'Federation', and six months later, on 22 January 1908, the British Brush Manufacturers Association was formed.[29]

Two men were instrumental in the formation of the BBMA: Ernest Kent of G.B. Kent & Company, the association's first president, and Charles Hamilton Watkins of Hamilton & Company (London) Limited, its treasurer. Both companies were old-established and well-respected. Hamiltons, in particular, were unquestionably the most prestigious manufacturers of paintbrushes.[30] Moreover, although their reputation was founded on top-quality, hand-made products, like Pages, they had always been at the forefront of progress. Indeed, in many ways their development had been similar. The company was founded in 1811 when Charles Foster Hamilton (1783-1856), a young journeyman brushmaker, set up his own business in Brick Lane, London.[31] In 1814, he moved to the Barbican and three years later to Banner Square; by 1836 he had settled with his family in Greek Street, Soho, the home of the business for more than fifty years (see plate 21). In 1838 he took as an apprentice Charles Adolphus Watkins (1823-1906). An enterprising young man, he studied mechanics and chemistry and in 1850 left brushmaking to join the Thames Plate Glass Company, set up to pioneer a new process for making mirrors. The business failed and Watkins' next venture was the manufacture of artificial manure, but in 1854, after 'two years of hard and unprofitable work', he returned to his old trade as a traveller for the Hawkins Brush Company.[32] And when in 1856 Charles Hamilton died, his widow, unable to cope with the growing trade, asked Watkins to manage it

Plate 18   Charles Foster Hamilton (1783-1856),   the founder of Hamilton & Company, and his wife.

Plate 19   Charles Adolphus Watkins (1823-1906), who adopted the trade marks Semper Idem, to demonstrate his commitment to high standards and consistent quality.

Plate 20   Charles Hamilton Watkins (1861-1925), managing director of Hamilton & Company, 1906-1925.

Plate 21 One of Hamilton & Company's early premises in Greek Street, Soho. The company was based in Greek Street for at least fifty years before moving to Clerkenwell in 1887.

for her. Two years later, after marrying her youngest daughter, Frances Harriet, he bought the business.

Watkins' inventiveness was quickly apparent. His first patent, for a soldered wire ferrule, was taken out in 1859.[33] A stream of others followed, among them, copper shoulders for wire-tied brushes (1871), seamless metal ferrules (1884) and improvements in graining tools and ferrules (1885). Moreover, Watkins trade mark, *Semper Idem* (always the same), adopted in 1867, emphasised the consistent quality of his products. Indeed, the *Building News* reckoned: 'Watkins' level bevelled varnish brushes surpass any other in the market for wear.'[34] Similarly, the range of medals won at international exhibitions - in 1879, Sydney, Australia, the following year, Melbourne, and in 1882, New Zealand - testify to success overseas.

Watkins' three sons, Charles Hamilton (1861-1925), Frederick (*c*.1862-1942) and Arthur (d.1930), all followed their father into the business which grew steadily. By the 1880s, the factory in Greek Street and a second workshop in nearby Rose Street, were cramped and outdated. A suitable site was found in Clerkenwell Road close to Farringdon Street station and in July 1887 a new factory was opened (see plate 24). The ground floor was lit by electricity which also provided the power for the lathes and machines for making Watkins' patent brushes which, according to the *Oil and Colourman's Journal*: 'have done much to revolutionise the painting brush trade.'[35] Like Pages, the factory incorporated its own engineering workshop. Several extensions were made to the works, but ten years later it was decided to move out of the city to Harrow where land was cheap and plentiful.[36] The move was accompanied by the introduction of new production methods so that instead of making the entire brush, each man carried out only one stage of manufacture. As with the introduction of machinery at Wymondham, these changes brought resistance from the workforce and a strike by members of the painting-brushmakers' union over 'automation and sectional methods of working'.[37] Undoubtedly, however, it was these developments which again enabled the firm to withstand the competition from abroad and make further advances.

In 1903 the business was registered as a private limited company with Charles Watkins as chairman and managing director

Hamilton & Co.,

No. 25.　Improved Varnish Tools.

3s.	4s.	5s.	6s.	7s.	8s.	10s.	13s.	16s.	20s.	26s.	doz.
1	2	3	4	5	6	7	8	9	10	12	Nos.

These are made of strong bristles, set in socket handle.

No. 26.　Flat Hog Hair Varnish, in Tin.

Polished Cedar Handles.

10s.	15s.	20s.	25s.	30s.	35s.	40s.	doz.
1	1½	2	2½	3	3½	4	inch.

These brushes are warranted sound for all varnishes and oils, but will not stand water.

No. 27.　Flat French Varnish, in Tin.

White Handles.

4s.	5s.	6s. 6d.	7s. 6d.	9s.	13s.	20s.	26s.	32s.	40s.	50s.	doz.
1	1¼	1½	1¾	2	2½	3	3½	4	4½	5	inch.

No. 28.　Scene Painters' Tools.

3s.	4s. 6d.	6s.	9s.	12s.	16s.	20s.	23s.	27s.	37s.	47s.	doz.
1	2	3	4	5	6	7	8	9	10	12	Nos.

Plate 22　Examples of brushes from Hamilton & Company's 1871 catalogue.

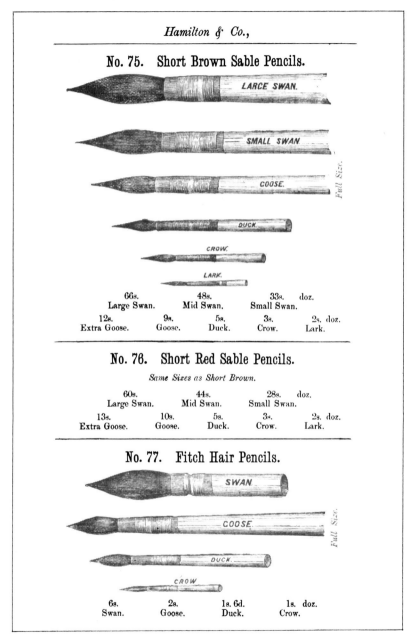

Hamilton & Co.,

No. 75. Short Brown Sable Pencils.

66s.	48s.	33s.	doz.	
Large Swan.	Mid Swan.	Small Swan.		
12s.	9s.	5s.	3s.	2s. doz.
Extra Goose.	Goose.	Duck.	Crow.	Lark.

No. 76. Short Red Sable Pencils.

Same Sizes as Short Brown.

60s.	44s.	28s.	doz.	
Large Swan.	Mid Swan.	Small Swan.		
13s.	10s.	5s.	3s.	2s. doz.
Extra Goose.	Goose.	Duck.	Crow.	Lark.

No. 77. Fitch Hair Pencils.

6s.	2s.	1s. 6d.	1s. doz.
Swan.	Goose.	Duck.	Crow.

Plate 23   A range of fine-hair brushes produced by Hamilton & Company in 1871

46

Plate 24 Hamilton's model factory in Clerkenwell Road, London, built in 1887.

and his three sons, directors. Barely three years later, Watkins died and shortly after, Frederick was forced to retire through ill health.[38] But Charles Hamilton, who took his father's place as managing director, clearly inherited much of his drive and inventiveness. Soon after the move to Harrow he successfully initiated the manufacture of flat varnish brushes, a field where previously the Germans had enjoyed a virtual monopoly.[39] At a time of crisis for the industry he instigated the formation of the BBMA and, finally, before the outbreak of World War One, had the foresight to introduce the American rubber-set process by which bristles were set in vulcanised rubber.[40] Initially both Hamiltons and Kents considered adopting the process and Arthur Watkins went to America to see at first hand its effectiveness. Two systems were considered, that invented by a Mr Firsichbaum, which was already used by several of the leading American brushmakers, and a cheaper process developed by a Mr Maywald. Kents decided against the venture, but in March 1913, the directors of Hamiltons agreed to buy two sets of Firsichbaum's machinery - only to find on their arrival they were so dangerous the

Plate 25 The Harrow factory, headquarters of Hamilton & Company, 1897-1990.

local authorities refused to allow their operation. Adjustments were made and the following year the Rubber Set Brush Company was registered as a subsidiary company.[41] Despite many early difficulties, the process was subsequently viewed as the most important breakthrough in the manufacture of paint brushes.

Plate 26 The interior of Hamilton's Harrow factory soon after its opening in 1897.

According to the trade journal, *Brushmaking,* by the outbreak of World War One, 'the British brush trade was a declining industry.'[42] Certainly, the number of small workshops diminished annually, while in his evidence to the Departmental Committee, W.P. Shave, the Norwich brushmaker, spoke of three firms, each employing upwards of a hundred hands, which had failed.[43] But in contrast, companies like Star Brush, Pages and Hamiltons, which had mechanised and introduced modern production methods, flourished. In each case, progress had been beset with problems: financial risk, strikes and technical shortcomings. Notably, Charles Page withstood

Plate 27   Hamilton's brushmakers, 1908, including three generations of the Goddard family (front row: 3rd, 4th and 6th from the left).

opposition from more conservative family members.   In his own words, he spent practically his whole life developing the business.[44] Similarly, until a few weeks before his death at the age of 83, Charles Watkins was engaged in experiments which would enable further mechanisation.[45]   Both, like Edward Bradley, were men of enterprise who were instrumental in driving through the changes necessary to meet the challenges of intensified competition in a free-trade world market after 1880.

NOTES

1.   *The Brush Journal,* Vol.III, No.4, June 1897, pp. 51-2.

2.   Dandy brushes were used for grooming horses and, to a lesser extent, dogs.

3.   Edward Bailey Page, 'History', pp. 3-4.

4.   The wholesale merchants who sold to retail shops were accused of secreting their suppliers' patterns abroad to obtain cheaper copies.   Charles Fountain Page, in his evidence to the Departmental Committee, gave

details of one consignment, imported from Austria, packed in boxes labelled with the name of a London manufacturer and stamped 'Warranted London Made'; *Report of Departmental Committee into the Importation into the United Kingdom of Foreign Prison-made Goods*, (Parliamentary Papers 1895), LXVIII, pp. 526, 588, 601-4.

5. Edward Bailey Page, 'History', p. 4; *Brushes and Toilet Goods,* November 1946, p. 30.

6. The work was completed by adding a false back which was smoothed and polished. A variation of drawn-work, trepanning, was used for working with ivory and for other high quality brushes. For a more detailed explanation of these methods see M.R. Snow, *Brushmaking*, pp. 65-74.

7. In 1805, the rate was 20 knots a penny in London, by 1872, 19, against 21 in Bristol and 22 in Sheffield. In 1866 the Manchester rate fell as low as 25 knots, in Ireland, 30. A 90 knot broom was considered a good job; working on small, 36 knot brooms was slower and therefore earnings were lower; W. Kiddier, *The Old Trade Unions,* pp. 119-125, 211.

8. The union threatened to withdraw their members from shops which employed women. A compromise was reached whereby members' wives could do the 'fancy' part of drawing. Kiddier suggests the numbers employed were small until the 1870s; W.Kiddier, *The Brushmaker and the Secrets of His Craft: his Romance,* (1923), pp. 66-7.

9. By 1910, Hawkins, in his survey of Norwich, recorded rates of up to 50 pence a week for girls, 60 pence for women, £1.25 for men and 'substantially more' for paintbrush makers. There remained only fifteen registered out-workers, who received 5-5½ pence per thousand knots, according to quality. He placed women brushworkers mid-way up the working class hierarchy: 'socially inferior to machinists in boot factories but decidedly above the worst-paid workers in laundries'; *Departmental Committee,* (PP, 1895), pp. 527, 588, 592, 603; C.B. Hawkins, *Norwich, A Social Study,* (London, 1910), pp. 46, 59.

10. M.R. Snow, *Brushmaking,* p. 29.

11. The evidence for this section is taken from T. Girtin, *In Love and Unity: a Book about Brushmaking,* (1961), pp. 41-45; *Brushes and Toilet Goods,* October 1936, pp. 2-3; Memorandum and Articles of Association and Register of Members, Star Brush Company.

12. *Departmental Committee,* (PP, 1895), p. 593.

13. £7,000 was paid immediately with the remaining £9,850 paid by instalments over the next fourteen years; Indenture for Purchase of Letters Patent, 10 March 1886; Norfolk Rural Life Museum, 602.974.1001.

14. Edward Bailey Page, Notes on the origin of the Briton Brush Company Limited, (Typescript), 1946.

15. Edward Bailey Page, 'History', p. 4; 'Notes on the origin'.

16. The cottages were bought from Robert Semmence who until that time had supplied the company's brush stocks and boards; Edward Bailey Page, 'History', p. 4.

17. The boiler-house, engine-house, finishers' and turners' shops and machinery were all destroyed; the Machine Room - containing the Gane machines was partially saved; *Eastern Daily Press*, 6 January 1890; *Norwich Mercury*, 19 July 1890.

18. S. Cherry, *Doing Different? Politics and the Labour Movement in Norwich, 1880-1914*, (1989), pp. 30-31.

19. The exception was in the painting brush department where the highest skills were required. Charles Page blamed trade union officials from London who stirred up local members and enticed workers to higher paid regions. He 'believed [trade unions] were the greatest curse on the country'; *Departmental Committee*, (PP, 1895) pp. 602-3.

20. Although there are no details, Charles Page also received financial support from his father, Samuel Deyns Page. Subsequently, he was excluded from Samuel's will: 'having already received a benefit from me in my lifetime.' Samuel left a mere £2,768, a further indication of the family's financial struggle during these years; Letter from E. Bailey Page, June 1950; Will of Samuel Deyns Page, proved 24 July 1897.

21. Reginald was educated at Felstead School, Essex, and Clare College and Ridley Hall, Cambridge. After incumbencies in Nottingham and Lincoln he became rector of Trimmingham, Norfolk in 1909. Cecil was educated at Norwich School and Corpus Christi, Cambridge (where he was Parker and Colman Exhibitioner) and St Bartholomew's Hospital, London. Unfortunately there are no details regarding Algernon and Edward, the latter may well have been trained as an engineer; Cox's *Who's Who in Norfolk*, 1912, pp. 191-2; *Eastern Daily Press*, 20 January 1903, 26 October 1951.

22. *Eastern Daily Press,* 24 March 1894.

23. *Departmental Committee*, (PP, 1895), pp. 600-3; *The Brush Journal,* Vol. 1, June 1895, p. 62, November 1895, p. 67.

24. The old brewery was leased for twenty one years at £60 per annum from Morgan's Brewery Company Limited of Norwich from 10 December 1896.

25. Burgess was similarly impressed by the slickness of the company's fire brigade, ably demonstrated by the manager, William Algar. Given recent events, this was perhaps not surprising; E. and W. Burgess, *Men Who Have Made Norwich,* (1904), pp. 144, 152-3.

26. The Museum Court factory was leased for sixteen years from 10 September 1903 at £160 per annum, including an option to purchase during the first seven years; File relating to an extension of the Company's works (1916), Norfolk Rural Life Museum, 602.974.988; Letter from E. Bailey Page, June 1950; S.D. Page & Sons, Price List, 1912.

27. Imports from Germany increased from 218,846 dozen to 686,579 dozen and from Belgium, from 409,007 dozen to 500,277 dozen; Annual Statement of Overseas Trade of the United Kingdom, 1900-1913.

28. *Brushmaking,* December 1923.

29. 'Something of the Work Done For the Trade by the BBMA', *Brushes and Toilet Goods,* July 1940, p. 85.

30. G.B. Kent & Company was founded in 1777 by a Yorkshireman, William Kent; Ernest Kent was the fourth generation of the family to enter the business.

31. Charles Foster Hamilton, the son of Francis Martin Hamilton, was in 1798 apprenticed to Richard Cripps, a paint brush manufacturer, of Duke Street, West Smithfield, London. He worked as a journeyman for two other firms before starting his business in Brick Lane.

32. Quoted from Watkins' diary in: 'Hamilton & Company (London) Limited', *Brushes and Toilet Goods,* April 1953, p. 45.

33. Ferrules: the 'case' which holds the bristle in place - originally made of wire, string or leather. Modern-day ferrules are made from stainless steel.

34. Quoted in T. Girtin, *In Love and Unity,* p. 40.

35. These included 'a large number of machines for tying brushes ... and a very ingenious machine [automatic in action] for making patent copper shoulders.' The machines for turning the oval handles were described as 'perfect pieces of mechanisation'; *The Oil and Colourman's Journal*, 1 August 1887, p. 1246.

36. A second reason for the move was the new fire regulations introduced by the London County Council after a serious fire in Smithfield. The cost of conversion was such that the entire manufacturing side of the business was moved to Wealdstone and only the sales department and offices retained at Clerkenwell Road; 'Messrs Hamilton & Company: A Great Paint and Varnish Brush House', *Brushmaking*, 17 April 1920, p. 161.

37. 'Messrs Hamilton & Company', p. 161; T. Girtin, *In Love and Unity*, p. 47.

38. The issued capital of the company was £30,000, which was increased to £42,000 the following year and to £50,000 in 1918. All the shares were initially held by the Watkins family. Walter Collett succeeded Watkins as chairman while Francis Geoghegan, the company's accountant, replaced Frederick as a director; Hamilton & Company (London) Limited, Memorandum and Articles of Association and Private Ledger.

39. Obituary of Charles Hamilton Watkins, *Brushmaking*, July 1925, p. 20.

40. The vulcanised rubber was impervious to the various substances in paint, varnish and distemper which damaged existing cements and, therefore, considerably extended their life.

41. Hamilton & Company (London) Limited, Directors' Minutes, 31 October, 3 December 1912, 6 February, 16 March, 18 December 1913, 3 September 1914.

42. *Brushmaking*, No. 1, Vol. 2, 20 January 1916, p. 3.

43. *Departmental Committee*, (PP, 1895), p. 588.

44. Will of Charles Fountain Page, proved 13 April 1921. His estate was valued at £82,142. He left 100 ordinary shares of £10 to each of his four sons, Edward, Algernon, Cecil and Reginald with the request that if they wished to dispose of them they should make every effort 'even at some personal sacrifice to sell them to one of their brothers so that [they] should continue to be held by members of my family.'

45. Obituary of Charles Adolphus Watkins, *Journal of Decorative Art*, February 1907.

CHAPTER III

The Amalgamation of 1920: The Briton Brush Company

World War One brought mixed fortunes to the brush trade. Almost immediately, most companies found their workforce sharply depleted as men joined up. In May 1916, the import of hardwoods such as beech, birch and elm was prohibited and the following month all trademarks, so crucial in home and export markets, were suspended for the duration of the war. Finally, bristle prices soared. On the other hand, huge government contracts restored prosperity to many companies. Certainly, Pages and Hamiltons, with their modern production methods, were soon heavily involved in war work. Hamiltons, for instance, were asked by the War Office to make shaving brushes and by 1916, despite the loss of a quarter of their labourforce, were delivering 50-60,000 brushes every week to the army.[1] Government contracts far outweighed the loss sustained in export markets. Moreover, because of the lack of continental competition, domestic sales, especially for cheaper brushes, were well maintained. Late in the war, the sale of brushes made by

Plate 28 Hamilton & Company's steam-driven van, 1916, which proved invaluable during the First World War when petrol was in short supply.

German prisoners brought complaints from the trade, but many companies clearly enjoyed healthy profits.[2]

Plate 29 S.D. Page & Sons' Haymarket factory, c.1900, with St Peter Mancroft churchyard in the foreground. The site is today occupied by the C & A store.

Most thoughts, nevertheless, turned to post-war reconstruction, the transition from war-work and the means to withstand a renewed flood of imports. This was particularly so at Pages. For whereas previously few firms could compete with their machine-made brushes, during the war, many smaller firms introduced machinery. Moreover, their out-dated city premises and, therefore, heavy overhead costs, meant they would struggle to compete in the post-war climate.[3] As early as 1916, then, plans were made to concentrate production. Several schemes were evaluated, all involving the closure of the old Wymondham Brewery and the transfer and extension of the drafting works to Lady's Lane. Again, these changes were necessary to compete with the specialist firms which supplied other manufacturers.[4] The options at Norwich included extending the Haymarket site by building a second factory along Church Street (see map) or, alternatively, purchasing and refitting Museum Court. Both were ruled out on cost grounds.[5] The preference was to replace the two with a new, single-storey factory built away from the city-centre, which would be more efficient to run and allow for future expansion. Again, cost, estimated at almost £30,000, was a prohibiting factor.[6] There remained, however, one final option: amalgamation, either with one or a number of companies.

Plate 30 The Briton Brush Company's private railway siding, opened in 1916 and closed fifty years later.

Some form of amalgamation had first been discussed in 1907 by those who proposed a federation of brushmakers. More serious attempts followed in 1917 when eight member-companies submitted accounts to the BBMA secretary and accountant, B. Marsden Till. Again, the scheme came to nothing. Subsequently, following an approach by Edward Bailey Page, Pages and Hamiltons held further discussions with a view to merger - the first of several occasions before the eventual amalgamation of 1990.[7] The proposals faltered, but the following year, Pages began merger talks with another London company, D. Matthew & Son. The business, founded in

1773 by James Smith of Fish Street Hill, was almost as old as Pages. In 1807 it passed to Smith's nephews, Henry and John Matthew who moved to 106 Upper Thames Street where the family traded for more than a century. In 1910, Frederick Matthew, the fifth generation, registered the business as a private limited company in order to raise finance to build a new factory and the following year D. Matthew & Son Limited moved to a spacious site at Tariff Road, Tottenham.[8]

The first directors of the new company were Frederick and his son Edmund (1878-1969). Frederick, with leanings to religious and academic pursuits, had little interest in brushmaking.[9] Similarly Edmund, his elder son, was something of a scholar and keen to continue his education at university. But at sixteen his father took him away from St Paul's School and brought him into the business. His brother Wilfred (1884-1918) - more of a sportsman - likewise left St Paul's at sixteen, but found himself a post in the Indian civil service where he remained for ten years until poor health forced his return. In 1910 he joined the business subsequently becoming a director. Sadly, he was killed in France shortly before the end of the war. By 1919 Frederick was also dead and the management of the company rested with Edmund and two working directors, John Sandy and Joseph Carpenter, who took responsibility for sales.[10] Edmund's ability was already apparent. The company, which employed almost three hundred, was, to quote Edward Bailey Page: 'forging ahead'.[11] It was noted in particular for its high quality pan-work and toilet brushes which were sold directly to large London retailers such as Selfridges, the Army & Navy Stores and Boots. Most brushes were hand-made, but Edmund had already begun the process of mechanisation having acquired a dozen machines of various makes; the only hurdle to his continued progress was a lack of capital.

There were several reasons why the merger was an attractive option for Pages. First, and most importantly, it provided the means of maximising the benefits of mass production while minimising the problems of standardisation. Traditionally, brushmakers made a wide variety of patterns which, of course, meant short production runs and high costs. Most buyers also liked to deal with a single firm. Therefore, too narrow a range meant loss of custom. However, by specialising in a smaller number of lines, the two companies between them could offer a full range of brushes at competitive prices. Second, in supplying Matthew's brush backs and handles, the sawmill (which operated on a time-work basis) could be worked to full capacity, thereby achieving further savings. Third, Matthew's valuable London connections would allow the new company to switch away from wholesale to retail selling. Last, but by no means least, was the need to strengthen the senior management of the company.

By the end of the war Page's board comprised directors who knew little about brushmaking. Charles, for so many years the driving force, had retired. His place as chairman and managing director was taken by Edward. But of the remaining directors, Robert Bagshaw (who had served the company in a non-executive capacity since its incorporation), and Edward's brothers, Reginald, Algernon and Cecil, only Cecil took an active role. However, he had no experience of the trade. Until 1915, when he joined the Royal Army Medical Corps, he worked in general practice in North Walsham. Invalided from the Dardenelles, he served for the remainder of the war at Shoreham as adjutant for Eastern Command, thereafter becoming a full time member of the firm.[12] Edmund Matthew would therefore clearly be a great asset to the new company. Nevertheless, despite his lack of business experience, Cecil was an able and perceptive man. Indeed, his understanding of the costs and benefits of merger did much to temper the enthusiasm of Edward, who believed that the new company, with its workforce of over 800, would become the premier brushmaking firm in England, able to sway the BBMA and the industry in general:

> There is a danger that other amalgamations will be formed in self defence. ... ... We are putting our feet on the bottom rung of a ladder that may be difficult and even dangerous to climb.[13]

Equally, though, he was wholehearted in his support: 'these are the days when one must go forward or go to the wall.'

In April 1920, at the height of the brief post-war boom, the industry's journal, *Brushmaking,* reckoned that 'never in the history of this ancient trade was the outlook brighter.'[14] Shortly after, S.D.

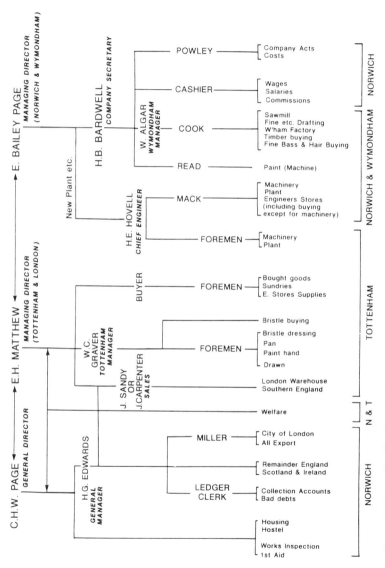

Figure 1 Edward Bailey Page's plan for the organisation of the Briton Brush Company after the amalgamation of S.D. Page & Sons and D. Matthew & Son in 1920.

Page & Sons was renamed the Briton Brush Company - a step taken to maximise the company's well-known Briton trade mark - and in June, the amalgamation with D. Matthew & Son was announced. By November, *Brushmaking* was noting the onset of depression.[15] And while the abrupt end of the restocking boom and the general recession were important factors, the underlying problem was again that of cheap imports. By the end of 1919, imports already exceeded the 1913 peak of 1.9 million dozen brushes by a further one million. In December 1923, imports stood at 3.8 million dozen, with Germany alone responsible for 1.9 million.[16] The reasons were twofold: the depreciation of most other currencies relative to sterling, making foreign goods more competitive, and wages which were well below those in England. Indeed, the situation was made more difficult because in 1919 the Ministry of Labour applied the Trade Boards Act to brushmaking, thereby fixing minimum rates for the trade. By 1923 wages for skilled men were £2.75 a week, compared to around £1 in Belgium with similar levels and differentials for women.[17]

The introduction of Trade Boards was of particular significance for the Briton Brush Company, for in 1920 Edmund Matthew was elected as President of the BBMA. Edmund, despite a reputation as a strict disciplinarian, enjoyed a good relationship with the unions. One of his first tasks as President was to represent the employers at the inquiry called in response to pressure from a number of firms to reduce wages.[18] His support for the men and insistence that 'no gentleman would wish to pay English workpeople the rates paid in Belgium' brought a storm of protest from the editorial of *Brushmaking*.[19] In fact he received much support and in 1923 led the industry's deputation to the Board of Trade which marked the beginning of a long fight to gain protection under the Safeguarding of Industries Act. At the local level, Cecil Page campaigned vigorously from the Conservative platform in the run-up to the 1923 general election; according to his opponents, the contest in South Norfolk could be summed up in the single word 'brushes'.[20] Doubtless he argued his case to its best advantage. Yet only when imports surged beyond the four million dozen mark and unemployment in the industry reached almost thirteen per cent, did the BBMA finally secure a Board of Trade inquiry into their case in

September 1925. The refusal to grant protection and the conclusion that depression in the industry was due more to the introduction of carpet sweepers than foreign competition brought the curt response from Edmund that: 'one almost regrets the Committee was not empowered to recommend a subsidy to the foreign manufacturers.'[21] The following year, his last as President, Edmund threw his weight behind a scheme for combination whereby a holding company and Board of Control would be empowered to oversee the rationalisation of production and distribution in the industry.[22] Despite, however, the greater co-operation fostered by the Association, few companies were prepared to relinquish their independence.

The reports of the BBMA demonstrate the scale of the problems. Those companies which had clung to the old ways quickly

Plate 31 Edmund Matthew (1878-1969), President of the BBMA, 1920-1926, and managing director of the Briton Brush Company, 1920-1949.

ceased trading and by 1926 even well-established firms such as C.H. Briggs & Company of Kilminster, had failed. Although the Briton Brush Company's survival was never threatened, the newly-merged company clearly struggled. Production was rationalised: Tottenham specialising in high-class hand-made brushes; Wymondham and Norwich concentrating upon machine-made ones. But far from increasing productivity, none of the factories worked at more than fifty per cent of capacity throughout these years.[23] In December 1923, Cecil Page wrote in desperation to the company's Australian agents, Lindsay Cormack, to explain why their prices were not so keen as previously. The company, he explained, had two options: to increase sales by acting as factors of foreign goods or to ship their idle machines to Australia (or elsewhere in the Dominions) and open a small factory.[24] The comprehensive report, sent in return to a request for information regarding the local industry, provided details of building costs, labour, raw materials and distribution in Australia. In spite of a willingness to be involved in the venture, Cormack's belief that 'Australia had enough Brush Making Machines to supply a population of 15 million instead of 5' deterred further action.[25] The company suffered a further blow when, in September 1924, the

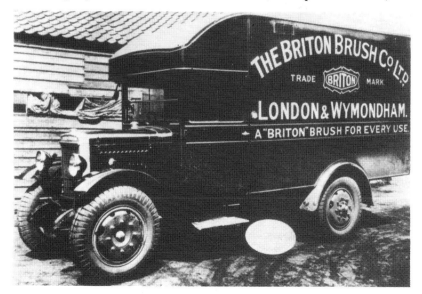

Plate 32 The Briton Brush Company's delivery van, c.1930.

Wymondham sawmills were gutted by fire. Overall, the decade was one of retrenchment. Despite the slow recovery of trade from the mid-1920s, the Haymarket factory was closed in 1927.[26] Two years later, Tariff Road, Tottenham was also shut and all production transferred to Wymondham.

The Wall Street crash and the world slump which followed brought further gloom to the industry. Imports reached new peaks, while the near collapse of G.B. Kent, one of the sector's leading firms, underlines the severity of the crisis. Only in 1932, after a long fight, did the industry at last receive protection when, under the Import Duties Act, a tariff of twenty per cent was placed on all imported brooms and brushes.[27] Almost immediately imports dropped sharply apart from a flood of cheap Japanese toilet brushes. Britain's early recovery, coupled with the boom in private house-building, did much to restore the domestic market, and by 1935 employment was rising as was the number of firms in the sector. Whereas in 1930 British firms captured only fifty-nine per cent of the home market, a few years later the proportion had risen to seventy-two per cent of an increased consumption.[28] The worst was clearly over.

Indeed, at Wymondham, where in 1922 the Co-operative Wholesale Society had also established a brush factory, these years were marked by a shortage of labour which threatened future expansion. As a result, every effort was made to streamline production. In 1930 George Marwood (1901-84), a young Cambridge engineering graduate previously employed by the Institute of Industrial Psychology was recruited. His appointment was opportune, for Edward Bailey Page, who had worked closely with the company's chief engineer, Herbert Hovell, in designing and patenting new products and machines, and who had been such a driving force in the company, was gradually forced to withdraw from active work through failing health. Already the company designed and manufactured much of its own machinery, but under Marwood the engineering and research departments grew to employ between thirty and forty skilled men. Among his many initiatives were the introduction of high-speed filling machines and, in 1935, the installation of a turbo generator which utilised waste wood to provide electric power for much of the factory.[29] That year, Edmund

Plate 33 George Marwood (1901-1984), who joined the Briton Brush Company in 1930 and retired as technical director in 1967.

Matthew also instigated a two-year time and motion study of the company - the first in the industry - which culminated in the appointment of another talented engineer, Fredric Wright (1903-1983). Born in South Wales, Fred, as he was always known, had studied chemical engineering at the School of Mines and pure science at London University. In 1928 he came to Norwich as assistant research engineer at Boulton & Paul, and four years later married Edward Bailey Page's only daughter, Dorothy. Laid off during the slump, he found posts in Lincolnshire and Manchester, before returning in 1937 to join the family firm. In 1934 the next generation of the Matthew family, Edmund's nephew John, (Wilfred's son), also entered the business. Educated at Haileybury and Trinity Hall, Cambridge where he read classics, John's first choice was the Colonial Service, with brushmaking very much second. As a complete newcomer to the trade, he found his greatest asset was his sporting prowess which ensured a rapid acceptance on the shop-floor. But his real training was with his uncle who took responsibility for buying the company's bristle. This was a key role, for most of the value of any brush lay in the bristle and an astute buyer who could second-guess the market on forward prices was

Plate 34 Fredric Wright (1903-1983) managing director of the Briton Brush Company 1949-1967, in his role as president of the BBMA 1954-5.

invaluable. And John, like Edmund, was to prove a good asset to the company.

The presence of the Co-operative factory also provided every incentive to foster a loyal workforce. Apart from the strike at the end of the nineteenth century, the company had always enjoyed good labour relations. Samuel Deyns Page was said to treat his employees as members of his family. His grand-son, Charles, despite his many difficulties, had in turn impressed a similar philosophy on his own son, Edward:

> No business has any right to expect success unless it renders service to the community [and] should only be carried on for the happiness and welfare of those who live out of it. ...[It] is a Trust of which each of us is a guardian and it is our duty to try and leave our particular work in a better state than we found it.[30]

Such sentiments were common. Most firms were family affairs and at the heart of labour relations was a paternalism which persisted late into the twentieth century. Examples abound: of summer outings, perhaps to Felixstowe or Skegness; of the Christmas bonus and, notably, in an age devoid of state support, of discretionary pensions.[31] In 1897, John Chamberlain, a London brushmaker, had left £10,000 to establish a trust for old and infirm members of the trade.[32] And at Hamiltons, a Workman's Provident Society, providing sickness, accident and death benefits to even the youngest of employees, was set up in 1899, more than a decade before the passing of the National Insurance Act.[33] Similarly, several firms encouraged their young apprentices to attend the Continuation Classes run jointly by the BBMA and London County Council.[34] Not surprisingly, long service was a tradition in the industry. Typically, the illuminated address presented to Charles and Arthur Watkins in 1911 to mark the firm's centenary was signed by thirty-one employees with at least twenty-years service and thirty-nine with more than ten.[35] By 1938, no fewer than 127, over a quarter of the workforce, had been with the company for twenty-five years. At Briton it was the same. May Squires, for example, was one of a family of eight who walked the three-and-a-half miles from Ashwellthorpe to work at Wymondham. Her husband's family, the Mabbutts, were likewise employed at the factory, and her sons, George, Cecil (Dido) and Billy, between them contributed 142 years to the company.[36]

The inter-war years brought further advances. Edward Bailey Page's plan for the organisation of the Briton Brush Company (see page 60) indicates his commitment to welfare. It was a concern shared by his fellow directors. Even in the difficult early 1920s, when funding for the Continuation Classes ceased, Edmund Matthew ensured they were maintained for the young workers at Tottenham.[37] He made it his policy to visit a different department every week and know every employee personally. At Wymondham, Cecil Page gave generously of his skills, providing free medical advice, a benefit, in a pre-National Health era, of immense value. Many workers enjoyed improved housing. Just prior to the merger,

Plate 35 Felling timber at the Checkendon Woodlands, Oxfordshire. Set in the heart of the beech-growing district, the woodlands were purchased by the Star Brush Company in 1920.

Plate 36 Loading the trunk of a beech tree onto the timber drug at the Checkendon Woodlands, Oxfordshire.

Plate 37 The Hamilton Star sawmill at Checkendon.

Pages acquired a further twenty-two acres adjoining the Wymondham factory. Here the company erected a number of cottages which were let at low rents. And after the closure of Tottenham, more houses to accommodate the London workers were built by the District Council on the Company's land at Preston Avenue. During the 1930s, the remaining land was developed as a sports ground. The athletic meeting held in July 1934, with the directors and their wives in attendance and tea provided for the employees' children, was the first of many such events. For many years the sports-ground was the home of a wide variety of clubs: football (Wymondham and District League champions in 1936-7), cricket, tennis, hockey and netball.[38] The company also boasted its own concert troupe and band - The Hurbs - which played for the dances regularly held in the clubhouse. Last, but by no means least in view of its history, was the highly efficient private fire brigade. All are evidence of a close-knit community and the company's success in promoting good labour relations during the inter-war years.

The period ended with a further setback, the war in China in 1937 adversely affecting the supply and price of bristle. The hardest hit were firms like Hamiltons which specialised in top quality paint brushes and used, on average, 120 tons of bristle a year. Many firms suffered, even the Star Brush Company, which catered for the cheaper end of the market, barely recording a profit in 1938. The

Plate 38 The Briton Brush Company's annual summer outing to Skegness, c.1935.

Plate 39 The 'making' shop at Wymondham decorated to celebrate the 1937 Coronation of George VI.

Plate 40 Hamilton & Company's football team, 1920.

following year brought a flood of orders for paintbrushes to cope with the blackout. Thereafter, the industry was on a war footing. Typically, at Briton, production was given over to government contracts ranging from shaving brushes to road sweepers for airfields.

As in World War One, the industry faced immense problems. The shortage of raw materials was exacerbated by the war in the Far East resulting in government controls defining the fillings for brushes made for the home-market. Equally serious was the shortage of labour. At Briton, well over a hundred employees, including two of the directors, John Matthew and Fred Wright, joined the forces.[39] More positive, however, was the Export Group set up by the BBMA in May 1940 to capture markets previously held by the Germans. Despite an acute shortage of shipping and the priority of war work, many firms reported record figures.[40] These were undoubtedly profitable years. At Star Brush, for example, annual net profits which averaged only £1,860 in 1938-9, increased to £25,842 in 1944-5, those at Briton, rising from £11,907 to £66,910 over the same period.[41] Such results clearly did much to dispel the gloom of the inter-war years and enabled the industry to plan for post-war reconstruction.

Plate 41 An aerial view of the Briton Brush Company's premises at Wymondham c.1930, showing the timber yard, sawmill, fibre dressing department and machine brush factory. The factory closed in 1985.

The Amalgamation of 1920: the Briton Brush Company

Plate 42   The Briton Brush Company's wood-yard, with Wymondham Abbey in the background.

NOTES

1. In 1916 Government contracts accounted for forty-one per cent of total sales. Exports, which in 1913 made up thirty per cent of sales, had fallen to fourteen per cent, mainly because of the shortage of freight transport. By February 1917, 112 of Hamilton's employees had joined the armed forces; Hamilton & Company (London) Limited, Directors' Minutes, 8 December 1914, 24 February 1916, 15 February 1917.

2. For example, Hamilton's annual net profits averaged £6,052 in 1910-13 and £6,277 (after allowance for excess profits taxation) in 1914-17.

3. 'A Scheme for the Amalgamation of S.D. Page & Sons Limited and David Matthew & Son Limited', Notes by Edward Bailey Page and Dr Cecil Page, December 1919.

4. The alterations at Wymondham also included demolishing four cottages facing Damgate Street and building new offices and rest rooms, extending the saw mill and trimming room. The new drafting works were completed in 1921; file related to the Extension of the Company's Works, 1916/17, Norfolk Rural Life Museum, 602.974.988.

5. The cost of extending the Haymarket factory was £24,949. This involved erecting a four storey extension, including offices, on the site of the

George & Dragon Public House, demolishing the stables and cottages to provide a concrete yard and factory entrance via Theatre Street (see map 1) and reorganising the old factory. The Museum Court extension, including the cost of purchase, was estimated at £24,749. Neither was considered a 'progressive or satisfactory development'; Extension of the Company's Works, 1916/17.

6.   To cover the cost and obtain pre-war profit levels required an additional return of £25,000. It was felt this was not possible 'in the face of the greater Home competition we shall certainly have after the war'; Extension of the Company's Work, 1916/17'.

7.   Hamilton & Company (London) Limited, Directors' Minutes, 15 February, 5 May 1917, 11 April 1918.

8.   D. Matthew & Son Limited was incorporated on 1 November 1910, with a nominal capital of £25,000; debentures of £10,000 were issued to finance the Tottenham factory; D. Matthew & Son Limited, Directors' Minutes.

9.   I am grateful to John Matthew for information about his family.

10.   John Sandy and Joseph Carpenter were appointed as directors in December 1911; they appear to have played little role in decision-making.

11.   'A Scheme for the Amalgamation'.

12.   Obituary of Dr Cecil H.W. Page, *Eastern Daily Press,* 26 October 1951.

13.   'A Scheme for the Amalgamation'.

14.   *Brushmaking,* 17 April 1920, p. 160.

15.   *Brushmaking,* 17 June 1920, pp. 253, 303; 20 November 1920, p. 480.

16.   Japan, a newcomer to the scene, added a further 660,000 dozen and Belgium, 551,740 dozen; Annual Statement of Overseas Trade of the United Kingdom.

17.   *Brushmaking*, December 1923.

18.   The Trade Boards fixed time-work basic rates and standard piece-work rates. The subsequent Cave Report agreed a sliding scale linked to the

cost of living index. The 1922 rates were 5 pence per hour (time-work) for unskilled men and 8 pence per hour for skilled.

19.   *Brushmaking,* March 1922, pp. 19-21.

20.   'Brushes and the Election', *Brushmaking,* December 1923.

21.   E.H. Matthew, Letter to *The Times,* 21 December 1925.

22.   *The Hardware Trade Journal,* 22 October 1926, p. 156.

23.   By October 1925, employees on hand-made brushes were working a three day week. To cut costs the proportion of female labour was increased and on average men were losing 19½ hours a week. By July 1926, unemployment in the industry stood at 20.4 per cent; among male labour employed on domestic brushes, 21.5 per cent; *Brushmaking,* October 1925, p. 39; *The Hardware Trade Journal,* 22 October 1926, p. 156.

24.   Letter from Dr Cecil Page to Lindsay A. Cormack, 27 December 1923; Australian Report, Norfolk Rural Life Museum, 602.974.1085.

25.   Letter from Lindsay A. Cormack to Dr Cecil Page, 27 May 1924. There is no evidence to show whether the company took the first option of factoring foreign-made goods - something it had never done and which was described as 'distasteful'.

26.   One reason for the upturn in trade in paintbrushes was the increasing vogue for tinted walls instead of wallpaper; *Brushmaking,* December 1926.

27.   A duty of ten per cent was initially placed on imported fibres but this was subsequently removed. Bristle remained exempt.

28.   Final Report of the Fifth Census of Production, 1935.

29.   George Marwood was previously employed by Garretts of Leiston, and married Dorothy, the daughter of Sir Frank Garrett. I am grateful to Michael Marwood for information about his father.

30.   Speech by Edward Bailey Page, *Brushes and Toilet Goods,* November 1946, p. 30.

31.   For example, in July 1914, 260 of Page's employees travelled by special train to Ipswich, then by boat to Felixstowe for lunch and back to Ipswich for tea.

32.   The Trust, administered by a committee of employers and workers, provided pensions of not more than £30 a year to retired and needy brushworkers who had been employed in the trade for at least twenty-one years. In the year ending March 1908, grants totalling £573 were paid to seventy-four pensioners. For many years Charles Hamilton Watkins served as secretary.

33.   The company contributed £100 a year. There were two scales of contribution; the lower, of 3d a week, entitled a member to ten shillings (50 pence) a week for sickness up to twelve weeks a year, a pension of five shillings a week and a death benefit of £7 10s; the higher rate of 6d brought double benefits. The scheme was dissolved in 1912 after the passing of the National Insurance Act which covered over 200 of the company's workers. The accumulated fund was used to build and furnish a Recreation Hall for the use of all employees; Hamilton & Company, Provident Society Rules; Directors' Minutes, 4 July 1912.

34.   The classes, held at the Polytechnic Institute, Clerkenwell, were attended by apprentices from Hamiltons, Matthews and G.B. Kent & Sons. They studied English, calculations, drawing, gym, dressmaking and carpentry and took part in inter-firm competitions; *Brushmaking,* 17 January 1920.

35.   Similarly, at the social evening held to celebrate the silver wedding of Edward Bailey Page, W.C. Graver, the Norwich manager, with forty-eight years service, presented him with an album signed by 370 employees. W. Lynch, with a record fifty-eight years service, presented Mrs Page with an inscribed silver tray; Norfolk Rural Life Museum, 602.974.895.

36.   I am grateful to George Mabbutt for information about his family.

37.   The cost of the classes was borne entirely by the company. In March 1922 the *Tottenham Herald* reported the performance of Oliver Goldsmith's *She Stoops to Conquer*, preceded by a one-act farce, *Keeping up Appearances*. 'The juvenile orchestra played selections in a manner which reflected the greatest credit on their training.'

38.   Since the 1890s Pages had fielded a football team which was begun by three apprentices, William Algar - by the 1920s, factory manager at Wymondham - and F. Brundell and T. Newall, both of whom subsequently played for Norwich City; *Eastern Daily Press,* 10 June 1949.

39.   Notably, Edmund Matthew, with the support of his wife, maintained a correspondence with every serving employee whom he could contact. Well over a thousand letters, many in his own handwriting, were

despatched to such destinations as El Alamein, Burma, Italy and Normandy. At the party held in 1946 to celebrate the company's 200th anniversary and to welcome back its serving men, the latter, as a mark of their appreciation, presented Edmund with a clock and his wife, a silver dish.

40.   Edmund Matthew served as chairman of the domestic brush group, and William Chadwick, the paint brush group; *Brushes and Toilet Goods,* August 1941, pp. 44-8.

41.   Pre-tax figures. Net profits at Star brush dipped to a low of £337 in 1938. Even when allowance is made for Excess Profits Tax, annual average profits increased from £995 in 1938-9 to £5,012 in 1944-5; File relating to the merger of Hamilton & Company and the Star Brush Company, 1954, Harrow Museum and Heritage Centre.

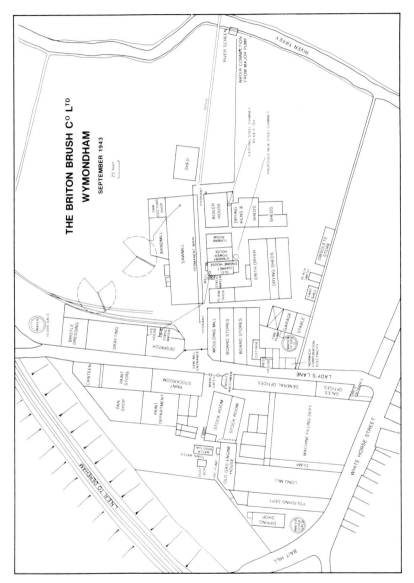

Figure 2 Plan of the Wymondham factory, 1943.

CHAPTER IV

Post-war Challenges and the Formation of
Hamilton Acorn Limited

When World War Two ended, the first problem for brushmakers was the adjustment to peacetime production.[1] Labour shortages persisted and restrictions on the use of bristle and imported timber remained in force. A number of companies also faced the prospect of extensive rebuilding. Few had suffered on the scale of Chadwick & Shapcott of Waltham Cross, hit in 1944 by a V1 and the following year by a V2 rocket, the latter causing the death of fifteen employees and injuries to around a hundred.[2] On the other hand, the desire of a war-weary nation to brighten their drab surroundings brought an immediate boom in sales of paint and domestic brushes. The industry also reaped the rewards of its war-time efforts overseas and by 1947 exports were almost double their pre-war level. Indeed, the profits bonanza of the war years was well maintained.

By 1948 trade had eased and thereafter brushmakers faced a number of challenges. First the export boom faltered as the need to preserve hard currency to finance reconstruction became a priority almost everywhere. Therefore, many countries placed restrictions on all but essential imports. As early as February 1947 New Zealand had introduced import quotas; in September 1949 the USA placed a fifty per cent tariff on several types of brushes while Australia, a major pre-war market, followed an embargo with variable quotas - by August 1954, sixty per cent of the 1950-51 level, falling to forty per cent the following year.[3] In response, British brushmakers formed foreign subsidiaries to manufacture and distribute their products. Hamilton set up and acquired a majority holding in two: Hamilton United Brush Company Limited, of Christchurch, New Zealand and, in 1950, Hamilton Brushes Africa (Pty) Limited of Johannesburg.[4] Similarly, in 1951 Briton acquired a fifty-one per cent stake in the Phoenix Brushware Company of Salisbury, Rhodesia.[5] Kents went to Eire and the Hollins Brush Company to Canada.[6] Generally, this proved an effective solution. At Briton, for example, the investment in Phoenix together with a network of foreign agents and sales tours by Fred Wright, maintained exports at around 25-30 per cent of total production, culminating in 1961 in the company's commendation by the Board of Trade for export achievement.[7]

Less easily resolved were the difficulties concerning the supply of bristle. Government controls ceased in October 1946 but brought little relief as political instability led to hoarding within China. Prices for the less favoured Indian bristle soared. Then, just as the situation in China eased, fears that the Korean War would cause more permanent disruption led to panic buying and further price rises. When in July 1951 the government belatedly reinforced controls (a measure taken to reduce the flow of dollars) the price of a standard case of Tientsin was £3.46 lb compared with £1.20 lb four years earlier.[8] Moreover, instead of adopting a quota system based on previous consumption as the BBMA had requested, the restriction limited the proportion of bristle used in manufacture. This proved especially damaging to companies like Hamiltons which supplied the quality paintbrush market. The subsequent slump in sales (an inevitable consequence of over-stocking by retailers) coupled with the sharp decline in bristle prices - by July 1953, Tientsin stood at £1.50 lb - resulted in the company facing losses averaging £18,670 in 1952 and 1953 with a further £40,000 written off stocks.[9] The experience was not forgotten. Most companies took advantage of low prices, particularly after 1956 when the UK and US governments released their stockpiles, and bought heavily. Hamiltons erected additional warehousing and always carried at least two years stocks. Nevertheless, the political situation and potential for the Chinese to exercise their monopoly position remained a threat for many years to come.

The quarter century after World War Two also saw unprecedented technical change. A major step forward was the establishment in 1946, in conjunction with Leeds University, of the British Brush Manufacturers' Research Association (BBMRA). Under the direction of Dr C.S. Whewell, the Association fulfilled two objectives: dealing with members' day-to-day problems and long-term research into raw materials and production methods. In an industry noted for its conservatism, it was to play a vital role in fostering a more open and co-operative environment and in the

Plate 43   Unloading imported fibres for brushmaking at the Briton Brush Company's railway siding at Wymondham, c.1950.

dissemination of technical information.[10]   Not surprisingly, given the persistent problems with the supply of bristle, much of its early work focused on the development of synthetic brush fillings.   The first of these, nylon, had been used to a limited extent during the war in the production of industrial and toilet brushes and by the 1950s was gaining wider acceptance.   However, for a number of reasons, including poor paint pick-up and uneven application, the early filaments were unsuitable for paintbrush manufacture.   Not until the

Plate 44 Mixing nylon fibres for hairbrushes at Wymondham, c.1950.

development of tapered nylon and the techniques of flagging and tipping were these problems sufficiently overcome to ensure a degree of acceptance.[11] Even so, it must be emphasised that bristle has remained the first choice for most professional painters. Similarly, plastic brush-backs and handles proved ideal for many household and toilet brushes and were quickly adopted. Yet paintbrushes were again a different matter. A number of small refinements, such as balsa wedges and metal inserts, were introduced,[12] but attempts to produce plastic handles were unsuccessful until the early 1970s. Only with the development of foamed polypropylene, which could be lacquered in the same way as wood, were plastic handles widely adopted.[13]

Hand in hand with these advances came the development of new setting cements. Leading the way was A. MacKenzie, a brush salesman who, in the 1930s, acquired a small brushmaking firm in Chesham (Buckinghamshire) from its bankrupt owner. Renamed

Amac Refinements after its new proprietor, MacKenzie quickly turned the company round and during the war perfected a process of plastic setting based on urea resin. The process, which speeded up manufacture and enabled the use of shorter and, therefore cheaper, sizes of bristle was initially used in pan-work in place of pitch. By the late 1940s a new company - Modern Brushware Limited - was registered to market the products and MacKenzie was offering a range of domestic brushes at less than half the normal price.[14] The major breakthrough came with the introduction of epoxy resin, a strong, hard cement more resistant to solvents than rubber and, therefore, ideal for paintbrushes. The process, developed in America by the Hardman Company, was not without its problems. Notably, when used with bristle, which swells when wet, the resin cracked. However, by the 1960s further work by Arthur Letts of Beck Koller (later Synthetic Resins Limited) in conjunction with the BBMRA, Hamiltons and Chadwicks, produced an acceptable resin which rapidly superseded rubber setting. The transformation of the paintbrush was finally completed by the adoption of stainless steel ferrules, pioneered by Hamiltons in the early 1980s.

A much wider range of machines was also introduced. For even in companies like Briton, among the first to mechanise, many

Plate 45 Trimming paintbrushes at the Wymondham factory, c.1950.

Plate 46 Sanding paintbrush handles at Wymondham, c.1950.

brushes were hand made. Generally, the only machines used in the manufacture of paintbrushes were those for turning handles and for nailing and trimming. Throughout the industry, such tasks as the preparation of fibre and bristle had changed little over the centuries. After World War Two, however, most companies felt the strain of rising wages and a growing labour shortage. Briton provided daily transport to Wymondham from nearby towns and villages like Watton and Hingham and paid wages sufficiently high to attract women from Norwich. To exploit a new source of labour and enable expansion, a small workshop was opened in the neighbouring market town of Attleborough. A site had been purchased in 1951 and a new factory for the production of paintbrushes built, initially employing around a hundred girls.[15] The previous year, under the auspices of the Anglo-American Council on Productivity, the industry sent a ten-man team to America. Led by Fred Wright, the team visited seventeen of America's leading brushmakers. Overall, they found productivity levels far higher than at home. Their conclusion that this was mainly attributable to a greater degree of automation clearly provided a further stimulus to British firms to follow suit.[16]

　　The leading companies were already introducing machines for sorting and mixing bristle. Indeed, Chadwick's had begun the process in the late 1930s and by 1946-7 had developed machines for their own use and for sale. At Briton, a range of machines - for knot-picking, filling and wood-turning - was designed and built in the company's workshops. Subsequently, the first fully-automatic machines were bought from specialist suppliers like the German engineering firm of Josef Baer. By 1959, Briton's local competitor, the Co-operative Wholesale Society, was operating a fully-automatic machine made by the Belgian company, G.B. Boucherie, capable of producing around 9,000 broom-heads a week.[17] Finally, from the early 1960s, automatic machines for making paintbrush heads, pioneered by Simms of New Brunswick, Canada, came into increasing use.[18]

These advances clearly did much to transform brushmaking. Equally important for the future of the industry, however, were the post-war changes in demand. First, it was soon evident that the market for household brushes - undermined by the widespread introduction of the electric vacuum cleaner - was not expanding. By the early 1950s, sales were little above the 1935 level, while in contrast, those of toilet brushes had increased fivefold, and of paintbrushes, by more than a half.[19] A decade later, these trends were exacerbated as many third-world countries, especially those with indigenous supplies of raw materials, set up their own brushmaking industries. Most produced the cheaper, household lines. Political instability in Africa, the major growth market, also left a legacy of debt problems. Therefore, by the early 1970s, the emphasis was shifting to the emerging markets of the Gulf States - where demand was for decorating, rather than household, brushes. Briton, for example, established a flourishing trade with Kuwait. Second was the change in the pattern of demand for paintbrushes. Traditionally, the market had focused on the professional painter. After the war, improved materials such as emulsion paints and greater leisure time, encouraged a shift to home decorating. The real stimulus came in 1953 with the formation of Polycell Products, for the company spent massively on advertising, exploiting to the full the new medium of commercial television. The result was the birth of 'DIY': new products, such as paint rollers, targeting the amateur market; a revolution in packaging and marketing and a shift from wholesale to retail selling. Finally, with the ending of resale price maintenance, the time-honoured relationship between representative and customer at last gave way to direct selling, mainly to national chains with the potential to dictate the market.

A final consideration for many companies was their ability to provide the capital and expertise to meet the challenges of the post-war era. Some family firms struggled to maintain succession; others simply ceased trading.[20] More commonly, the way forward was through merger and rationalisation. In the autumn of 1951, the directors of Star and Briton opened negotiations to amalgamate the two firms.[21] Their objective was to merge, form a publicly-quoted holding company and invite other firms to join, in particular, John Palmer Limited of Portsmouth, with whom Star jointly-owned the Diss brushmaking firm of Aldrich Brothers.[22] Both Briton and Star were concerned about their future management. Bernard Bradley, who had succeeded his father, Edward, as managing director of Star had died in 1945. Leslie Shadbolt who joined the board as long ago as 1919, became managing director and, in 1948, chairman. Of the remaining directors, none had technical or production experience. Similarly, at Briton, Dr Cecil Page, the chairman, was seventy-two. Neither of his sons had entered the business. Only the managing director, Edward Bailey Page's son-in-law, Fred Wright, had maintained family succession; his only son, Peter (1933-1990), was eighteen. On the Matthew side, Edmund was seventy-three and his nephew, John, appointed to the board in 1948, was the last family member to join the business. In financial terms, Briton was the stronger.[23] Star, with its reliance on a narrow range of household brushes, was clearly more disadvantaged by post-war changes in demand. However, the company was in the final stages of purchasing a fifty per cent stake in Amac Refinements and Modern Brushware and, with it, the rights to MacKenzie's plastic setting process. Moreover, both companies were cash-rich - Briton holding massive reserves in excess of £350,000. Indeed, a key reason for seeking a public quotation was to ease the burden of death duties and enable family shareholders to realise the true value of their assets. But for the untimely death of Dr Cecil Page in October 1951, the merger would almost certainly have taken place. He was succeeded by his son, Philip (a forestry consultant) as chairman. Despite the support of the Matthews and Fred Wright, the Briton board was evenly divided. The financial control of the Page family - unable to avoid death duties - carried the day.[24]

Disappointed in their mission, the Star Brush Company turned to Hamiltons. On 1 February 1955 the two firms merged. The objectives were similar to those which had prevailed four years earlier: to secure continuity of management and gain economies of scale in purchasing and production. To combat the shift to DIY, Hamiltons were also introducing a range of products designed for the amateur market. And Star, while they had not resolved their problems of diversification, had well-established links with retail outlets. The chairman of the new holding company, Hamilton Star Limited, was Kenneth Watkins (1894-1989), Frederick Watkins' son and the fourth generation of the founding family. He was joined by Lesley Shadbolt and Cecil Kerr, the company secretary at Star. Initially, the two companies maintained their identity, with Watkins joining the Star board and Shadbolt, Hamiltons. However, four years later, after a lengthy work-study analysis by a team of outside consultants, Star's Holloway factory was closed and all production concentrated at Harrow.

In an increasingly competitive climate, the merger of Star and Hamilton was typical of many others. In 1960, Briton acquired the Neeta Brush Company of Fleet, Hampshire (which had developed a process similar to that of Amac) and, the following year, W.H. Vowles & Son of Stonehouse in Gloucestershire.[25] A capital stake was also taken in Dosco of Cork. Undoubtedly, however, the most significant merger of the period was the acquisition in 1960 of Chadwick & Shapcott by Polycell Products Limited. Chadwicks was another old-established, family concern, founded in 1866 by Sidney Chadwick (1843-1910), a young West Country brushmaker who travelled to London and set up in business in Blenheim Road, Holloway.[26] In 1908, after a brief partnership and several changes of address, Sidney merged his interests with those of Albert Macey (1868-1952), the proprietor of Edwin Shapcott & Company who, besides factoring Shapcott's wares, manufactured hand-made marbled wallpapers and painting brushes. To mark the amalgamation, a new trade mark - the well-known acorn - was registered and adopted for the high-quality paintbrushes for which the firm steadily gained a fine reputation.[27]

Plate 47 Chadwick & Shapcott's factory at Waltham Cross, built in 1936 and closed in 1973. The site is now occupied by Sainsbury's Homebase.

In 1908, Chadwick & Shapcott was also incorporated as a private limited company, with Albert Macey and Sidney's son, William (1875-1957) - who had entered the family business at the age of twelve - as joint-managing directors. The business expanded rapidly, moving from its Durham Road site to Henry Street, off the Grays Inn Road, in 1914, then in 1936 to a five-acre site at Waltham Cross in Hertfordshire. During the war, William Chadwick in his role as president of the BBMA, worked closely with the Ministry of Supply in maintaining essential bristle supplies to the industry. Described by his obituarist as a man of gentle charm and sincerity, he was awarded the OBE for his outstanding contribution.[28] His two sons, Leonard and Peter, followed him into the business; Leonard as bristle buyer and Peter taking responsibility for research and development. The Macey family completed the management team: Albert's son, Sidney, who had joined in 1908, and his grandsons, Stuart, Desmond and Richard. Therefore, when Polycell sought to complete their range of 'Poly' decorating products, it was not surprising that they turned to Chadwicks. Indeed, the result was a highly successful combination: Chadwick's manufacturing expertise and Polycell's marketing skill.

In 1965, however, Polycell was itself taken over by the Reed Paper Group. Reed had recently acquired the Wall Paper Manufacturers Limited which, besides such well-known companies as Crown Paints and Sandersons, included the Hollins Brush Company of Darwen, Lancashire. Hollins, a wholly-owned subsidiary formed in 1939 to complement the parent company's product range, like Chadwicks, made high-quality paintbrushes. The two companies were therefore merged into Chadwick Hollins and production concentrated at Waltham Cross.[29] Subsequently, the desire to increase market share led Reed to Briton and, in March 1967, a bid of £725,000 was made for the whole of the share capital of the company.

The offer for Briton came at a time when the company was seeking to consolidate its interests further. The previous year had seen a second attempt to merge with Hamiltons. The move had been agreed in principle - only to fail when outside consultants advised that Briton shareholders should receive two thirds of the shares in the new company. Expansion at Attleborough had continued, with extensions in 1957 and the mid-1960s, maintaining the company's position at the forefront of the trade. Indeed, in 1967 Briton led the export field, accounting for a quarter of UK total exports of paint and household brushes.[30] However, the Wymondham factory, much of it built around the turn of the century, was by now outdated and

Plate 48 William H. Chadwick OBE (1875-1957), managing director of Chadwick & Shapcott and president of the BBMA 1941-1944. The portrait (by Maurice Codmer) was commissioned by the Association to mark his outstanding contribution to the industry during the war.

Plate 49 Chadwick & Shapcott's trade stand at the Building Exhibition, Olympia, in 1955, featuring their Acorn trade mark. Visitors were shown film slides of brushmaking at the Waltham Cross factory.

inefficient. Plans to re-fit the factory had been drawn up in the 1950s, but not implemented, mainly because of Fred Wright's cautious attitude to investment. For while there was no questioning the management expertise - itself an attraction to Reed - the problems of family succession evident in the 1950s had not been resolved. Fred Wright's son, Peter, had brought new blood into the firm; otherwise there were few active participants. On the other hand, the family maintained financial control. The Reed takeover, therefore, provided the essential capital injection while enabling family shareholders to realise their assets.

The takeover clearly marked a watershed in the history of the Briton Brush Company. Peter Page Wright was quickly promoted within the Reed Group, leaving the company and bringing to an end the long tradition of family ownership and paternalistic management. In its place, the corporate culture brought a revolution in financial policy, sales and marketing, matched only by the unprecedented changes facing the industry. Notably, John Cheston, who joined Briton as sales manager in 1963, transformed the firm's representatives - the bowler-hatted 'gentlemen of the road' - into a modern sales team. Subsequently, as managing director, 1979-88, he led the company through some of its most challenging years. Similarly, Peter Chadwick, an acknowledged world-expert on paintbrush technology, firstly rationalised the product range at Chadwick Hollins then, after the merger with Briton to form Briton Chadwick, applied his skill and expertise to the new company. Thus by 1973, all paintbrush production was concentrated at Attleborough and the factory at Waltham Cross closed. Three years later, reflecting the shift to polypropylene and cheap wood imports, the Wymondham sawmill was also closed. Moreover, whereas the market for paintbrushes, influenced by the steady growth of home-ownership and DIY, remained buoyant, that for household brushes dwindled further. Despite heavy investment by Reed and a greater emphasis on cheaper lines, the company was unable to compete with import dumping by Far East competitors. In 1978-9 imports more than doubled over the previous year and, reminiscent of earlier times, the chairman of Briton Chadwick, Walter Giles, called for fair competition and castigated the government for its support of foreign industries based on an underpaid work-force.[31] Finally, in 1982 the company ended its enduring links with the town of Wymondham: the household side of the business was sold by Reed, subsequently becoming the Windmill Brush Company.[32] Five years later, Reed sold its paint and DIY products division to Williams Holdings and, in 1988, Briton Chadwick was renamed Acorn Decorating Products.

Plate 50 Hamilton's delivery van, 1961.

For most of this period, Hamiltons had remained very much a family firm. After the death in 1925 of Charles Hamilton Watkins, his brother Arthur took over until his own death five years later. He was succeeded by his wife Dorothy (1874-1975), who remained a director until well into her nineties; even then, she was regularly to be seen at the many social functions organised by the company. The last of the Watkins family to enter the business was Frederick Watkins' son, Kenneth, who began his career as a shipyard apprentice in the navy. He served as director, 1927-42, and chairman, 1942-75, subsequently becoming the company's first president. In 1958 he received the MBE for services to brushmaking. Generally, the remaining directors were drawn from long-standing employees. Miss Mabel Mercer joined the company in 1902, becoming secretary to Charles Hamilton Watkins, company secretary, 1925-55 and, from 1931, director. Similarly, Fred Claye began as tea boy in 1927 and retired as managing director fifty years later while Bob Clarke, the last indentured apprentice in brushmaking, ended his career in 1991 as technical director.

Plate 51 Dorothy Watkins (1874-1975), a director of Hamiltons for more than 40 years, with her nephew, Kenneth Watkins MBE (1894-1989), a director, 1927-75, chairman, 1942-75 and president, 1975, at the dinner in 1961 to celebrate Hamilton's 150th anniversary.

However, if the character of the company changed little, it faced the same challenges as did Briton. Further subsidiaries were acquired: in 1960, the small business of H.G. Goody of Hornsea, producers of fine-hair brushes; in 1969, E. Atkinson & Son of Dronfield, Sheffield, who made putty knives and scrapers and, three years later, J.T. Millwoods of Norwich, an old-fashioned concern making high-quality wall-brushes.[33] Two overseas companies, Hamilton Brushes of Canada Limited and, in 1963, the London Brush Company of Sydney, Australia, were also established. In 1971 there was a third attempt to merge with Briton - on this occasion thwarted by the Reed board. Four years later, however, despite continued modernisation, the directors noted a 'steady decline in the company's share of the market, both in volume and value.'[34] A major problem was falling exports to the Congo. In addition, Hamiltons suffered from the ascendency of the national chains and the shift to own-brand products. The demand for household brushes continued to decline steadily culminating in the closure of the Star Brush section. And like Briton, Hamiltons were forced to alter their policy of self-sufficiency and buy-in cheaper, imported wood handles. Thus in 1982, the woodshop at Harrow and the Checkendon sawmill were closed with the loss of fifty-three jobs. The following year, Blundell Permoglaze acquired a fifteen per cent stake in the company and, early in 1985, purchased the remainder of the shares. Within a few months however, Blundell was itself acquired by the Dutch company, Akzo, which did not include Hamiltons in its expansion plans. Therefore, under the leadership of the managing director, David Gordon, six of the directors staged a management buy-out. In September 1989, they sold Hamiltons to Lionheart plc. The last event in the story was the acquisition the following year of Acorn Decorating Products by Lionheart. Thus in 1990, Lionheart finally brought together some of Britain's best known and oldest established brushmaking concerns to form Hamilton Acorn Limited.

The present-day company of Hamilton Acorn marks the culmination of two-and-a-half centuries of brushmaking. These years have witnessed many notable milestones: the coming of the railways which transformed local markets; exports sent to every corner of the world and mechanisation which, in the 1890s, brought a bitter wave of strikes but proved essential in the fight against import dumping. Similarly, the persistent problem of bristle supplies prompted an on-going search for new materials, from Bahia bass to the synthetic filaments of the modern era. All these changes together with the oscillations of the trade cycle, especially in the 1880s and the inter-war years, tested the resilience and foresight of the seven generations of the Pages, the Watkins, Bradleys, Matthews and Chadwicks whose family firms are the ancestors of Hamilton Acorn. Between them they included many of the leading figures of the brushmaking industry: innovators such as Edward Bradley and Charles Adolphus Watkins, who risked their own and their company's futures, sometimes, as in the case of Charles Fountain Page, in the face of

Plate 52 Dennis Marrison (centre), managing director of Hamilton Acorn, with past members of the company pictured during a visit to the Attleborough factory in 1996, the year of the company's 250th anniversary, left to right: Peter Chadwick, John Cheston, Douglas MacDonald, Michael Marwood, Bob Clarke and George Mabbutt.

fierce family resistance; Edmund Matthew and Cecil Page displayed a business philosophy founded upon a deep commitment to the well-being of their workforce. If, in this modern world, their paternalism seems out-dated, in its day it fostered a close-knit and caring community - an enduring strength in many a family firm. Last, but by no means least, was the contribution of the workforce, just as with the owners, generation following generation. Their dedication, hard work and loyal service was equally outstanding. This brief history provides a tribute to them all.

NOTES

1.   Typically, at Briton, between 1939 and 1945 government contracts accounted for more than eighty per cent of total production; *Eastern Daily Press,* 9 April 1954.

2.   The company was also one of the few to be bombed in World War One when the factory, then in Henry Street, Grays Inn Road, Holborn, was hit by a Zeppelin; *Brushes,* August 1961, p. 36.

3.   *Brushes,* February 1947, p. 28; April 1955, p. 27.

4.   Hamilton & Company (London) held a fifty-seven per cent stake in the New Zealand enterprise while Hamilton Brushes Africa was jointly owned (Hamilton fifty-two per cent) with National Brushware (Pty) Limited. The managing director of Hamilton United Brush Company Limited was E.C. Munt, son of J.W. Munt, who had trained at Hamiltons in London before emigrating to New Zealand in 1908. He set up his own business - J.W. Munt & Company - in 1922, then merged with two companies to form the United Brush Company Limited. While serving in the RAF during the war, E.C. Munt approached Hamilton, resulting in the New Zealand subsidiary; *The Press,* (New Zealand) 13 February 1968.

5.   Over the long term this proved to be a very profitable venture, the investment of £5,000 returning annual dividends of £2-3,000.

6.   *Brushes,* December 1952, p. 65; March 1955, p. 55.

7.   *Brushes,* September 1961, p. 27.

8.   In four years the value of stocks increased from £157,000 to £388,000

requiring an additional £230,000 of capital; Hamilton & Company, Chairman's Report, 22 November 1951.

9.   The value of sales fell from £726,648 to £476,852 in 1951-2. The company was also hit by the embargo on imports into Australia; Hamilton & Company, Chairman's Report, 9 December 1952, 9 December 1953.

10.   Funded by the industry, the Association was administered by a council of brushmakers, chaired for many years by Fred Wright. Besides Dr Whewell, it had a full-time staff of three research chemists. By 1952, there were 109 members and that year it dealt with 152 enquiries from fifty different firms. The 1956 British Productivity Council thought: 'the measures to promote better co-operation undertaken by the BBMRA are among the most valuable developments in the industry ... more than any other step [the Association] has contributed to the increased efficiency in the industry in recent years.' *Brushes,* July 1952, pp. 60-65; September 1956, pp. 48-54.

11.   The filaments are tapered to resemble bristle; it is this characteristic which causes the paint to flow towards the tip as the brush is pressed and worked. The working tip of the fibre is also ground to a fine, soft point or mechanically split (flagged) to resemble the tip of bristle. I am grateful to Peter Chadwick for details of the technical changes in brushmaking.

12.   Wedges: packing strips to tighten bristle in the ferrule before cement is added. These impart taper and improve paint-flow. Balsa-wood is particularly suitable because it is soft and crushable and allows the brush to swell inwardly when wet, thereby avoiding distortion. Metal inserts are U-shaped pieces of aluminium, buried at one end in the epoxy setting and nailed to the handle through the ferrule, thus adhering the bristle securely to the handle.

13.   Paintbrush handles are still commonly made from beech wood. The advantage of rigid foam plastic is that the handle can never swell or shrink according to moisture changes or be ruined by excessive soaking.

14.   T. Girtin, *In Love and Unity,* pp. 100-06; *Brushes,* May 1949.

15.   *Eastern Daily Press,* 9 April 1954;

16.   Anglo-American Council on Productivity, *Productivity Team Report on the Brush Industry,* (1950), p. 43. The productivity team was the first from a small industry to visit the US under the scheme. The team also included W.A. Gosling, a bristle dresser and pan hand at Wymondham, and C.T. Mitchell, engineer and technical adviser at the Star Brush Company.

17. Two further machines were ordered; 'Re-planning and Automatic Machines Raise CWS Factory Output', *Brushes,* December 1959, pp. 24-7.

18. Simms made automatic machines for their own use in the 1930s. The first to be used in Britain was purchased by the Hollins Brush Company *c.*1962.

19. *Brushes,* February, 1948, p. 58; February 1952, pp. 36.

20. Typically, the firm of Bidwell, Bidwell & Company Limited, founded in 1839 and specialists in hand-drawn, bone-brushmaking, ceased trading in 1955. After several setbacks, including the loss of three directors in four years, the board announced they were unable to carry on the business any longer; *Brushes,* September 1955, p. 32.

21. This section is based on letters between Edmund Matthew and Lesley Shadbolt, 12 October - 17 December 1951.

22. Albert Leng and his brother Arnold (of Christopher Leng), both of whom were approaching retirement, were known to be interested. Neither had children, but with a nephew in the business, were concerned to diminish death duties and secure its succession.

23. Briton returned average annual pre-tax profits of £105,000 in 1946-51 on an issued capital of £119,107, the Star Brush Company, annual profits of £22,895 on an issued capital of £75,000 over the same period.

24. As a private company, the shares were assessed for death duties against the full value of the company's assets. Shortly before his death, Dr Cecil Page, the major shareholder, transferred his holding to his son - but too late to avoid death duties. The company remained private until its acquisition by Reed.

25. W.H. Vowles, founded in 1836, was first acquired by William Butler & Company (Bristol) Limited in 1954. The company was purchased by Briton for £40,000. The Stonehouse factory was closed in 1969. For details of the company's history see: 'A visit to Vowles of Stonehouse', *Brushes,* July 1951, pp. 50-53.

26. I am grateful to Peter Chadwick for information about his family. See also: 'Paintbrushes for Professionals and Do-it-Yourself Trade', *Brushes,* August 1961, pp. 35-39.

27. Until 1925, Chadwick & Shapcott manufactured a full range of household brushes and, until 1958, industrial brushes. The acorn - derived from William Chadwick's belief that 'great oaks grow from little acorns', remains the trade-mark of the present-day company of Hamilton Acorn.

28. *Brushes,* December 1955, pp. 33-5; August 1957, p. 21.

29. The Hollins Brush Company was established at Queen's Mill, Darwen, moving to a modernised factory in a former weaving mill, Marsh House Mill, in 1947. This was closed in 1966, subsequently becoming industrial units. See also: 'Famous Brush Houses, No.18: Hollins', *Brushes,* March 1950, pp. 60-1.

30. *Norwich Mercury,* 17 March 1967.

31. WPM News, May 1979; in 1980, the company produced 12 million brushes, of which 9.5 million were paint brushes; the Attleborough factory, which extended to 7½ acres, employed 190 people.

32. The Windmill Brush Company went into voluntary liquidation in 1985, when the Wymondham factory was finally closed. The site became a private housing estate; the only reminder of the factory which for almost a century was Wymondham's major employer is the road named Briton Way.

33. H.G. Goody was closed and production moved to Harrow; similarly, after a few years, Millwoods was closed and incorporated at Harrow. Atkinsons continued to be managed by Glyn Atkinson, grand-son of the founder, as a subsidiary company. I am grateful to Bob Clarke for this information.

34. Hamilton & Company (London), Directors' Minutes, 12 November 1975.

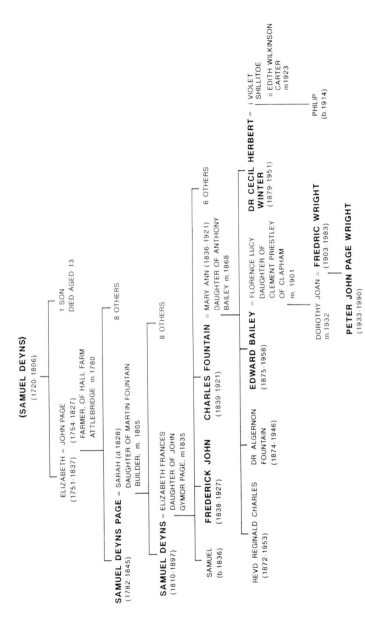

(SAMUEL DEYNS)
(1720-1806)

ELIZABETH = JOHN PAGE
(1751-1837) (1754-1827)
FARMER, OF HALL FARM
ATTLEBRIDGE m.1780

1 SON
DIED AGED 13

SAMUEL DEYNS PAGE = SARAH (d 1828)
(1782-1845)   DAUGHTER OF MARTIN FOUNTAIN
BUILDER, m. 1805

8 OTHERS

SAMUEL DEYNS = ELIZABETH FRANCES
(1810-1897)   DAUGHTER OF JOHN
GYMOR PAGE, m1835

SAMUEL
(b.1836)

FREDERICK JOHN
(1838-1927)

CHARLES FOUNTAIN = MARY ANN (1836-1921)
(1839-1921)   DAUGHTER OF ANTHONY
BAILEY m.1868

8 OTHERS

6 OTHERS

REVD REGINALD CHARLES
(1872-1953)

DR ALGERNON
FOUNTAIN
(1874-1946)

EDWARD BAILEY = FLORENCE LUCY
(1875-1958)   DAUGHTER OF
CLEMENT PRIESTLEY
OF CLAPHAM
m. 1901

DR CECIL HERBERT = i VIOLET
WINTER   SHILLITOE
(1879-1951)   ii EDITH WILKINSON
CARTER
m1923

PHILIP
(b.1914)

DOROTHY JOAN = **FREDRIC WRIGHT**
m 1932   (1903-1983)

PETER JOHN PAGE WRIGHT
(1933-1990)

The Page Pedigree: the names of those involved in the company are shown in bold

103

Index